Teaching Beyond Spoken Words

Communicating With Bilingual Nonspeaking Children in the Classroom

Lilly Padía

Foreword by Mariana Souto-Manning

Teachers College Press
Teachers College, Columbia University

Published by Teachers College Press,® 1234 Amsterdam Avenue, New York, NY 10027

The research referenced in this book was partially funded by the New York University Steinhardt Doctoral Travel and Research Grant, in the amount of $900, in Fall 2021.

Front cover design by Edwin Kuo. Illustrations by Virinaflora / Shutterstock.

Library of Congress Cataloging-in-Publication Data is available at loc.gov

ISBN 978-0-8077-8698-7 (paper)
ISBN 978-0-8077-8699-4 (hardcover)
ISBN 978-0-8077-8302-3 (ebook)

Printed on acid-free paper
Manufactured in the United States of America

To my first class of kindergarten students, who taught me more than academia ever did or could; Achilles, Emmanuel, Joshua R., Joshua V., Max, and Sebashton: This is for you.

Contents

Foreword *Mariana Souto-Manning* ix

Acknowledgments xi

Introduction 1

Defining the Terms 1
The Status Quo: Problematic Current Practices 5
Centering Children, Families, and Educators 8
Communicative Justice Takeaways 11
Overview of Chapters 12
Teaching in Action 14

1. None of Us Is Free Until All of Us Are Free 17

"Listening" to All Forms of "Speaking" 17
Key Idea(s) 18
The Status Quo: Problematic Current Practices 20
Learnings from Children, Families, and Educators 24
Communicative Justice Takeaways 26
Teaching in Action 28
Planning for Communicative Justice in Your Daily Lessons 31

2. Expansive Theories of Communication 33

Communication Requires Collective Commitment 33
Key Idea(s) 35
The Status Quo: Problematic Current Practices 42
Learnings From Children, Families, and Educators 44

Communicative Justice Takeaways 46
Teaching in Action 52

3. Beyond the Bilingual Confusion Trope 57
Forced to Choose: Bilingualism or Monolingual Special Education 57
Key Idea(s) 58
The Status Quo: Problematic Current Practices 59
Learnings From Children, Families, and Educators 60
Communicative Justice Takeaways 73
Teaching in Action 74

4. "We Make Our Own Systems" 79
Nonspoken Communication Systems in the Classroom 79
Key Idea(s) 80
The Status Quo: Problematic Current Practices 83
Learnings From Children, Families, and Educators 83
Communicative Justice Takeaways 95
Teaching in Action 96

5. Intent to Communicate and the Perceiving Subject 105
Expanding What "Counts" as Communication in the Classroom 105
Key Idea(s) 106
The Status Quo: Problematic Current Practices 109
Learnings From Children, Families, and Educators 110
Communicative Justice Takeaways 122
Teaching in Action 123

Conclusion 133

References 137

Index 143

About the Author 153

Foreword

(Re)Imagining Language as Limitless

What if language were limitless—not confined to speech, but alive in every form of expression? Imagine a world where communication flows freely, not bound by a single mold or standard. In this world, every gesture, every movement, every look holds meaning. Lilly Padía's *Teaching Beyond Spoken Words: Communicating with Bilingual Nonspeaking Children in the Classroom* invites us to step into this world, where communication is as diverse as the human experience itself. In this world, every form of expression is honored—not just tolerated, but deeply valued.

Padía calls us to pause, to reflect, and to shift our perspective on teaching, learning, and connection. She asks us to see language not as something fixed, but as something that evolves with life—fluid, multifaceted, and endlessly creative. In this reimagined world, nonspeaking bilingual children have profound ways of communicating that deserve not just our attention, but our respect. Their voices, in all their forms, are already here, waiting for us to listen with open hearts.

At the heart of *Teaching Beyond Spoken Words* lies the wisdom of families. Through the stories of four bilingual nonspeaking children, Padía shows us that families—out of necessity and love—are creating innovative, personalized communication systems. These systems are not born from a desire to "fix" or "cure," but from the deep human impulse to connect. These families are not just navigating a system; they are reimagining it, showing us that true connection is found not in conformity, but in the willingness to see each person in all their complexity.

Padía's work invites us to let go of rigid expectations about communication. She shows us that it's not about fitting children into predefined molds, but about expanding our understanding of how people can express their thoughts, needs, and dreams. Every gesture, symbol, and word is an opportunity to understand the richness of human experience. Through Padía's lens, we learn that the act of communication is never static—it is a living, breathing exchange that has the potential to reveal deeper truths about one another.

This book is a call to action, but it's not a call to impose change—it's a call to listen. Padía invites us to hear not only the words spoken aloud, but also the unspoken layers of meaning that exist in every form of communication. She offers strategies rooted in empathy, creativity, and openness—not just for educators, but for anyone who cares about the dignity and potential of every child. When we open ourselves to diverse ways of expression, we create spaces where all children—regardless of how they speak or how they don't—can truly be seen and understood.

Teaching Beyond Spoken Words urges us to reimagine language as expansive, inclusive, and deeply human. It asks us to honor the intrinsic value of every form of communication. It encourages us to learn from the families who have already paved the way—creating systems of connection that are meaningful and personal. The book is an invitation to rethink the way we relate to each other, to language, and to learning. It's a call to build classrooms where every child's story is heard, where every child can thrive in ways that reflect their unique humanity.

Padía's message is simple yet profound: Every child has a story. And every story deserves to be heard—whether through spoken words, symbols, gestures, or technology. *Teaching Beyond Spoken Words* opens up a world of possibilities, showing us that when we broaden our understanding of communication, we create spaces where all children can find their voice and their place.

This book is not just a theoretical exploration. It is a practical guide. Padía offers concrete tools, strategies, and resources to help educators cultivate and sustain classrooms that honor the diverse ways children communicate. Through the "Teaching in Action" sections, Padía provides us with actionable insights to integrate the communication systems children and families have developed into our own practices. By listening with empathy and being open to new ways of knowing, educators can unlock the full potential of every child.

Teaching Beyond Spoken Words is more than a book—it's a movement. It calls us to unite in cultivating learning environments that are inclusive, connected, and compassionate. Padía challenges us to imagine a world where communication is not a barrier, but a bridge—where every voice is celebrated, every child's story is heard, and every child's humanity is honored.

This book is a roadmap for change—a guide to creating spaces where every child can be heard, understood, and empowered. When we embrace the limitless possibilities of communication, we not only transform classrooms—we transform the way we relate to each other as human beings.

Now is the time to act. Let's come together to create a world where every child can communicate in ways that reflect their full humanity—where every voice is heard, and every story is valued.

—Mariana Souto-Manning, Ph.D.
President, Erikson Institute

Acknowledgments

First and foremost, I thank my parents, Thomas Padia and Julie Bernstein, and my sister, Tasha Padia, who engaged with me in true and expansive communication partnerships from the very beginning: My commitment to communicative justice stems from you three. To my grandmothers, both of whom were public school teachers: I strive to live in your legacy every day. To my brilliant and supportive committee and readers for the study that prompted this book, Erin O'Connor, María Rosa Brea, Heather H. Woodley, María Cioè-Peña, and Erica Saldívar García, who always kept me centered on the work and the community, rather than the gatekeeping milestones: I remain in academia with hope and love because of you; this work remains grounded in its purpose of liberation for children, families, and educators because of you. To my T3 Dream Team at Erikson: Sandra Osorio, Meghan Green, and Ja'Re Thorn, teaching and learning with you through this writing process has been the ultimate gift. To all my colleagues at Erikson, and especially Mariana Souto-Manning, Luisiana Melendez, Crystasany Turner, Luis Bernard, Amanda Moreno, Sam Melvin, Jessica Miguel, Jeanette Banashak, Seulki Ku, Crystasany Turner, and the FSJP Erikson Chapter, thank you for guiding me and holding me in community. My deepest gratitude goes to Emily Spangler, María Paula Ghiso, Donna Alvermann, and all the editorial team at Teachers College Press for their feedback and support in making this book come alive. Thank you to my colleagues and friends Christine, Hollie, and Melissa, who read chapters and gave me feedback from their experiences on the ground. Thank you to my various writing accountability partners as I saw this book to fruition: Jed Kuhn, Litzy Galarza, David Stovall, and Pamela D'Andrea Martínez. To my students: You remind me why we do this work. Thank you for your unwavering love for our children, for wading through the murky waters of the school system with me toward justice. To all my colleagues and supervisors at P168X: The Success Express in the Bronx, NY, and especially to Ms. Ana Zambrano—thank you for teaching me the ropes and hopes of special education. Endless gratitude to my partner, Vladimir Andrew Holly, who affirmed and fed me every step of the way as I wrote this manuscript into existence. Finally, to my daughter, Selma, who was growing inside me as I saw this book to the finish line: May you grow up in a world where communicative justice is realized.

Teaching Beyond Spoken Words

Introduction

> "Another world is not only possible, she is on her way. On a quiet day, I can hear her breathing."
>
> —Arundhati Roy

This book centers the experiences of bilingual nonspeaking children—children who do not communicate with vocal speech—and their families to highlight how dynamic language use occurs outside of school spaces. The hope is that this work can shed light on communication practices that may not be recognized, supported, or encouraged in school spaces, to move our learning spaces toward affirming and understanding all forms of communication and expression that our young people practice. "Teaching beyond spoken words" refers to the ways educators can learn from young nonspeaking children and their families to carry their communicative practices into formal learning spaces, including but not limited to the classroom. When we commit to carrying the knowledges and languaging that happen at home into formal schooling, we must be cognizant that these physical places are often designed like prisons and discourage an expansive, joyful, holistic expression of self in their very design (rows of desks facing the front, physically imposed hierarchy and rigidity, etc.). Learning from children and families to teach beyond the spoken word is not just about picking up a habit or a practice from a child's home life and depositing it inside the physical classroom; rather, carrying over community is about engaging in collective transformation, in becoming the most comprehensive, thoughtful, and connected communication partners possible in every space we co-construct together.

DEFINING THE TERMS

I use *nonspeaking* rather than *nonverbal* when discussing the young people in most of this book. Many advocates and self-advocates prefer the term nonspeaking to nonverbal, because nonverbal implies that someone is without words; nonspeaking people have words—they just do not speak to communicate them (Riggs, 2021). Some nonspeaking people use communication devices, including alternative and augmentative communication (AAC) devices; some use picture symbols; some write or type to communicate; some use other means. AAC devices are supports that may be used as tools of expression for nonspeaking children. They are often electronic tablet-like devices programmed with visuals that a child can tap or select, and have the device "speak" the word(s) via auditory output. AAC devices, then, are used as tools to move a nonspeaking child's communication closer to that which is typically perceived by a speaking and hearing society. AAC use, while a tool that is certainly helpful to its primary user, is ultimately a tool meant to accommodate the receiver and to move the "speaker" more in line with status quo spoken communication. Because an AAC device is used as an extension of a child's communication, it is considered a form of their "voice."

Writing is a verbal act, and some kids write or use verbal language that is not spoken but is still verbal. Many disabled activists who do not speak to communicate prefer to use this term as well. This distinction between nonverbal and nonspeaking has slowly started permeating popular culture. In *Happiness Falls*, a novel that came out in 2023, author Angie Kim explains that the main character Eugene, a teenage boy with multiple disabilities, does not speak but that this does not mean he is not verbal. He can read, and he is learning to communicate in ways others might understand by using a particular letterboard system. All of that is verbal communication, though it is not vocal or spoken. Despite the push to move to nonspeaking, these terms persist in our professional spheres and so at times I use them to refer to the labels that are used in educational settings.

I use *bilingual* and *multilingual* to refer to individuals and families who communicate using more than one language. At times I use the term *emergent bilinguals labeled as disabled (EBLADs)*, coined by María Cioè-Peña, to refer to students who are both becoming bilingual and labeled as disabled. I use the term *languaging* to refer to language as a verb and the embodied, co-constructed nature of language use (Brea-Spahn & Bilingual Language and Literacy Investigative and Networking Group, 2023; Maturana, 1978). I use the term *translanguaging* to refer to the ways that multilingual people communicate using their full linguistic repertoire. Translanguaging is discussed more below. I use the terms *special education* and *disability* to refer to the labels and programs assigned to children in our formal schooling systems. Some scholars write the term with a slash, like *dis/ability*, to highlight the false binary between being disabled and being "abled." I use both person-first language (i.e., a person with a disability) and identity-first language (i.e., a disabled person) at different times depending on the terms the participants used for themselves.

In defining the terms of the field and in this project, I want to foreground the ways in which labels reify hegemonic norms. Django Paris (2019) reminds us of this when he writes about terms like *urban* and *at-risk* that are used to name students of color while simultaneously avoiding naming race or racism. These codes and labels are used to other anyone who fits outside a white, middle-class, monolingual, ableist norm in our schooling system.

While many of the terms used in formal schooling and medical pathology to describe children are deficit-oriented, my goal is for all of us educators to both unpack and transform the language and the structures that maintain these deficit ideologies.

Schools are often positioned as the utmost experts on who children are and what they need, with school and school-adjacent professionals providing recommendations to parents/caregivers of children that their families are expected to accept with gratitude and deference. The assumption that schools are acting in the best interest of children and that school professionals have more knowledge and informed expertise than children themselves and their caregivers is rooted in white supremacy and patriarchy. Families have rich communication practices that are rooted in love, empathy, and affirmation. Learning from these practices, as opposed to the medicalized, white supremacist norms that govern schooling, can teach us all how to move toward liberatory languaging. *Liberatory languaging* is the idea that language and communication are tools to help people express and exist as their truest selves, in their most unrestricted, most free form. This is in contrast to the ways that language is often used to constrict, confine, and direct how people are allowed to express themselves, and what types of language are recognized and honored as valid forms of expression. Liberatory languaging encourages and understands all forms of expression as valid and valuable. Tara Yosso asked us "Whose culture has capital?" (2005). When we consider families of nonspeaking young bilingual children and the communication practices they create and enact, we can see rich cultural capital that exists outside the bounds of what is recognized by the larger system of schooling. These families are engaged in freedom dreaming (Kelley, 2002), envisioning and actively working toward a world where everyone is free and the systems that currently confine and constrain us no longer exist. Communicative justice and liberatory languaging (Brea-Spahn & Bauler, 2023) are being increasingly discussed in the context of bilingualism and multilingualism. How we expand conceptions of communicative justice to integrate inclusive education with bi/multilingual education and language education has critical implications for nonspeaking bilingual young people and for all of us as interconnected, relational beings (Cioè-Peña, 2021b; Sins Invalid, 2019). Working toward communicative justice in our classrooms is also an invitation and reminder that all educators are language teachers and all people—including educators—are lifelong language learners.

It has become a common practice in academia to write "positionality statements" to foreground our work. Much in the same way that many organizations have started issuing land acknowledgment statements to recognize the unceded Native land that we live and operate on, positionality statements often seem like performances of "wokeness" rather than deep interrogations of how power operates. Rather than just sharing a laundry list of our multiple identities separated by commas (Evans-Winters, 2023), recognizing how I am positioned in relation to the work I do and the people I work with, and constantly revisiting, reflecting on, and paying attention to how the power dynamics influence my work, is crucial (Boveda & Annamma, 2023). That being said, my positioning in this work has many layers. I am a white and Latina (Russian-Jewish, German-Swiss, Mexican-American) woman from Oakland, CA who uses English and Spanish. This impacted my experience throughout this research because families often slipped into Spanglish or moved between English and Spanish as we were communicating. I am a former public school teacher who spent most of her adult life and teaching career in the Bronx, NY, where my maternal grandmother was born and spent her early childhood. This showed up in the research because parents would ask me questions or for advice regarding special education services or programs in New York City—which I happily answered, in the hopes that the research project benefited not only myself as the researcher, but provided access and information to the families who so generously shared their time and stories with me. I am primarily nondisabled, though I experience anxiety and depression, which in some situations puts me on disability checklists. As an adult, I have experienced migraines that leave me temporarily unable to speak (temporary aphasia) and impact my ability to see clearly. This identity is particularly important because my shifting relationship to disability has also shifted my relationship to the work and the families who shared their own disability and language experiences with me. For example, the days and weeks following an experience of temporary aphasia, I was much more fixated on the bodily experience of being nonspeaking than the weeks when words flowed vocally out of me like water.

Finally, in this moment, I recognize that I am a person with a terminal higher education degree; I have a PhD. Throughout the process of this work, several of the parents in the study would say something and then qualify it with, "But you're the expert, what do you think? Is my child developing like they should?" What I told them, and what I hope to highlight for all of us in this book, is that my degree does not make me the expert. I firmly believe that families are the experts of their own experience, and within that, children are the utmost experts of their own experience. My job, and our job as adults who love and care about these children and families, is to build communication practices and pathways that enable us to fully understand and follow the expertise, guidance, and experiences of children and families.

THE STATUS QUO: PROBLEMATIC CURRENT PRACTICES

I began my career as an educator in District 75, New York City's public special education program for students with moderate to severe disabilities. I knew going into the New York City Teaching Fellows—a program that aims to bring people from various backgrounds and careers into the field of education and retain them—that special education was one of the highest-need areas for that year, so I was likely to be assigned to special education. I had no experience in special education or disability, aside from my own family and personal experiences with depression and anxiety, and family experiences with chronic pain and illness. I opted for District 75 because the bulk of what I thought I knew about special education related to disproportionality and the overrepresentation of children of color in special education programs in the United States. I figured that if I were in D75, chances would be that the students genuinely needed and could benefit from the programming provided. What I found both affirmed and challenged this assumption.

My first several years as a classroom teacher, I taught students in kindergarten through 5th grade, all of whom were labeled with autism spectrum disorder. Many of my students did not use spoken language to communicate. For this reason, I discuss people using language, rather than speaking it. The school system refers to students who do not speak as nonverbal. Many of my students also came from homes where English was not the dominant language spoken. As a Spanish user myself, for my students who used Spanish, I was able to informally assess their expressive and receptive language skills—a framework dictated by the school curriculum at the time—across the formal language systems of English and Spanish. However, I had never been trained in the pedagogy of language learning, and I grew increasingly concerned that we were not adequately supporting our students who were multilingual and nonspeaking. For example, if a student was evaluated by the speech-language pathologist and it was determined that she needed an alternative and augmentative communication (AAC) device, those devices were always programmed exclusively in English. An AAC device is typically something like a tablet that is programmed for a student to select pictures, images, words, or to type, and then the device will produce an audio output. It is important to note that even the name of the communication supports—"alternative and augmentative"—implying that there is something deviant about forms of communication that rely on these devices, and further reifies spoken named languages as the norm (Nair, 2022). A *named* language is a language officially or formally recognized by institutional powers like nation-states. Not only were my bilingual students' devices always programmed in English, but they were also always programmed in an adult's voice, rather than a child's voice—which is odd and important to note because these devices are supposed to be an extension of a child's voice, so it would follow that the audible vocal voice would be developmentally appropriate to sound like a child.

Time and time again I received professional developments and advice that "An AAC device is an extension of a student's voice. It should travel everywhere with them. Their voice shouldn't turn off at the end of the school day or when the bell rings at the end of class. It should go to the cafeteria, to the bathroom, home, etc. with the young person." For my students whose families did not use English, if they had devices that were not programmed to communicate in the language(s) their families used, we were cutting them off from developing and using their voice with their families.

I went back to school 2 years after receiving my Masters of Science in Teaching (MST) in special education to get my Bilingual Extension. I became increasingly concerned with not only how we distinguish between cognitive disabilities and language acquisition, but also with how to best support and honor the wholeness of our students living at the intersections of disability and language development. The U.S. schooling system, with its use of standardized testing and "universal" instruments like the Common Core or Next Generation Learning Standards, has a preoccupation with typical development; anyone who deviates from this normative standard is marked as delayed, deviant, or inferior. For students living at the intersections of emergent bilingualism and disability, there is often a preoccupation with *which* delay/deviance is dominating the student's development. I aim to reframe the conversation to move away from a deficit perspective of both language and disability and instead focus on how we can center and honor the developmental and communicative realities of young people.

After 7 and a half years of classroom teaching and working as an instructional coach with students in special education in grades K–8, it became clear to me that this intersection needed attention, and not just in my school. Students who are multilingual and nonspeaking deserve pedagogy that honors their multimodal, multilingual meaning-making. While my initial concern was about language difference versus language disorder, it ultimately led me to this work on expansive communication and literacies. Even thinking about language "differences" often positions difference in relation to a norm, rather than considering a spectrum of expression. Instead of thinking about dichotomizing between language differences versus language disorders or disabilities, I instead choose to focus on the rich communicative practices that bilingual nonspeaking students and their families engage in, in the hopes that I can offer up a guidebook for educators to learn from these children and their families to fully honor students' full selves and range of communicative abilities in learning environments.

According to the U.S. Department of Education, over 650,000 students are both identified as English learners and have Individualized Education Programs, or IEPs (U.S. Department of Education, 2022). There are no data on how many students in special education across the country are nonverbal or nonspeaking, which makes this dynamic all the more difficult to address. Within individual schools that support students with intensive and extensive support needs, administrators, teachers, and related service providers can often tell you which kids are nonverbal at the school, but those data are not systematically captured or recorded anywhere. One may initially think to look for students with a speech and language impairment (SLI) on their IEP, but the truth is that SLI is often identified for kids who are speaking but demonstrate some delays with their vocal speech in the context of a neurotypical, monolingual control group that is measured using normative scores from hegemonic standardized assessments. An IEP is a legal document that outlines a student's disability diagnosis and their designated special education services, accommodations, strengths, needs, and goals for learning. It is updated every year. Often students with autism spectrum diagnoses are those who fall into the nonverbal/nonspeaking category, but again, this information is not documented in any common way. This makes it difficult to identify how many students across the country are being underserved, because the numbers on them simply are not collected/do not exist in that way. *But if one child is being harmed by our school system and how the status quo currently operates, that is one child too many.*

The "problem" that I address in this book is how (little) we attend to the full communicative repertoire of our nonspeaking bilingual children. Too often their classes are in English, their communicative devices and systems are taught and/or programmed in English, and/or their related services like speech therapy are in English. Typically, goals on their IEPs or Individualized Family Service Plans (IFSPs) center on getting the child to develop spoken English language, ignoring the multiplicity of ways these children express themselves (e.g., gesture, facial expression, body language, eye gaze, use of assistive technology, drawing). Often, bilingual or multilingual children with disabilities are directed into monolingual English classes and services under the logic that bilingual instruction is too confusing for students. There are no data to back this up, and yet this myth continues to be perpetuated and enacted in schools. The problem is multilayered, then, but ultimately, I would like to situate the problem within the systems, structures, policies, and practices of schools. The problem is not with how the children communicate; the problem is with how schools set up communication structures that marginalize and obscure the communicative practices of nonspeaking bilingual students.

CENTERING CHILDREN, FAMILIES, AND EDUCATORS

As ideological approaches to multilingualism have led to the expansion of dual language and bilingual programs in public schools, bilingualism and language learning have entered the spotlight in pedagogical discourse. Within the context of learning English as a new language and bilingual education, the theory of translanguaging provides opportunities for students to use their full linguistic repertoire to communicate (García & Wei, 2013). Traditional linguistic and psychological theories claim that bilingual people have two distinct linguistic repertoires that they switch between. Translanguaging challenges these theories to rethink the way our brains and selves experience language; translanguaging posits that bilingual and multilingual people have one linguistic repertoire that houses all one's linguistic tools for meaning-making. Studies examining translanguaging focus on ways to honor a student's full self, including multiple modes of meaning-making (City University of New York–New York State Initiative on Emergent Bilinguals, 2017). Scholars in the fields of both bilingual education and special education have focused on the importance of distinguishing between language acquisition challenges and cognitive disability for school-aged children. There is also a small field of emerging scholarship examining translanguaging in the context of special education classrooms (Cioè-Peña, 2017; Przymus & Alvarado, 2019), but almost no studies to date have examined the translanguaging practices of emergent bilingual students with disabilities who are nonspeaking (O. García, personal communication, November 21, 2019). Students who are nonspeaking are in the unique position of communicating in ways that are often misunderstood or disregarded in school settings. Because nonspeaking students communicate in ways that are often outside the bounds of hegemonic communicative practices, there has been very little focus to date on the translanguaging practices of emergent bilingual nonspeaking students. I conducted a yearlong study exploring how translanguaging is experienced by young nonverbal emergent bilingual students with disabilities when interacting and communicating with their families. Data were collected through family/home environment observations, and semi-structured interviews (Seidman, 2019) with students, parents/guardians, and educators.

Educators committed to culturally responsive and sustaining education (Alim & Paris, 2017; Ladson-Billings, 1995) often consider issues of language learning, multilingualism, and differentiated instruction to be central elements of socially just teaching and learning. While bilingualism or multilingualism is viewed as an asset for students who are (often white and) dominant in English and acquiring a second or other language, students of color for whom English is not their primary language are viewed through a deficit lens (Flores & Rosa, 2015). This manifests in students being labeled with terms like "English learners" and placed in programs that prioritize the learning and proficiency of English. These policies persist, despite the fact that the United States has no official language. Language learning scholars and educators have moved away from terms like English learner and instead use the term *emergent bilinguals* (EBs) or *emergent multilinguals* (EMs) to highlight that students are in the process of becoming bilingual or multilingual (García & Wei, 2013).

For emergent bilingual students with disabilities, the best approach to language learning and instruction is hotly debated. Some students and families are advised by medical and/or educational professionals that learning two languages simultaneously is too confusing for students with disabilities to handle (Yu, 2016). Genesee (2016) conducted a review of the literature on bilingualism for "at-risk" students and found that evidence supports all students' participation in bilingualism programs. Many schools do not explicitly denounce bilingual education for emergent bilingual students with disabilities, but simply do not have the certified teachers and/or programming available. For all these reasons, many emergent bilingual students with disabilities end up in monolingual English special education settings. Extensive research focused on the disproportionate representation of emergent bilingual students in special education suggests that diagnostic tools are often inadequate and lead to the misdiagnosis of emergent bilingual students in special education (Harry & Klingner, 2006).

While emergent bilingual students with disabilities are being considered more frequently in the realm of language learning and bilingual education, students with the most significant and intensive support needs continue to be largely left out of language pedagogy discussions. Students who are nonspeaking communicate using a range of methods, from eye gazing to gesturing to drawing or writing to using alternative and augmentative communication (AAC) devices or picture-based communication systems (Picture Exchange Communication Systems, core boards, etc.). Emergent bilingual students with disabilities who are nonspeaking often receive what are considered some of the most intensive special education services in some of the most restrictive class settings (e.g., a range of individualized related services like occupational therapy, speech-language therapy, physical therapy in small classes, where the ratio is often as small as six students to one teacher and one paraprofessional [6:1:1]). To date, very few studies have focused on the translanguaging experiences of emergent bilingual nonspeaking students (Cioè-Peña, 2021b).

This book explores the languaging practices of bilingual nonspeaking students with disabilities, ages 3 through 9. The study that this book derives from entailed a combination of observations and ethnographic fieldnotes (Emerson et al., 2011) of children with their family members, as well as interviews with nonspeaking bilingual children, their caregivers, and their educators. I share anecdotes from my own classroom teaching experience that have some fictionalized details to ensure full anonymity of the people involved. The anecdotes from my own classroom teaching as well as the stories from the families and children in the study all use pseudonyms; any identifying names and information have been altered to protect their identity. Families play an integral role in a child's communication and literacy development. They are often the people who spend the most time early on communicating and interacting with a young person. However, in school settings, families are too often positioned as non-knowers, while school professionals or medical professionals are situated as the experts with the answers when it comes to communication development. Understanding how communication—particularly translanguaging—occurs between family members of nonverbal/minimally verbal/nonspeaking children can offer insights for school systems that too often push the outdated narrative that monolingual English instruction is the least confusing for dis/abled bilingual children. While nonverbal and nonspeaking are terms used most often to describe children who do not use oral speech to communicate, *minimally verbal* (what I also refer to as *minimally speaking*) is a term used by some educational professionals and caregivers to describe children who use very limited spoken words to express themselves. Minimally verbal or minimally speaking people often use one or two word phrases and/or may repeat words that are spoken to them or that they have heard on television, but are generally considered to use limited spoken language to express their own thoughts.

This book emerged from work that I did with nonspeaking bilingual children and their families. It includes both case studies from a research project and reflections from my own experiences as a classroom teacher. In many ways, I continue to benefit from this work more than anyone; not only am I learning about these children and their families, but I am learning about myself. For example, when I did interviews with mothers of nonspeaking bilingual children, several of them mentioned the "magical" connection that their children had with one another, and how they were able to communicate in ways the adults could not. I realized that this was the case with me and my sister when we were younger; we would often communicate with each other in ways our parents could not comprehend. I have also learned ways that I did not sufficiently notice, ask about, or open myself up to nonverbal, unspoken communication when I was a classroom teacher. I offer anecdotes from my own teaching at the start of each chapter, and in almost every example, my research with nonspeaking children and families has helped me realize how much I did not know when I was a new teacher. This book is not about feeling bad for the ways we misunderstood or misconstrued our nonspeaking bilingual children; it is about what we can learn from them and how we can use that knowledge to create better, warmer, fuller learning experiences for all of us. What I hope to offer teachers, families, and children is a bridge between homes, schools, and school systems to help uplift and amplify the expertise of bilingual families of nonspeaking children. During my research, I also offered support to the families in the study wherever I could; for example, I discussed options of public special education programs with one mother, sharing information on bilingual programs having no negative effect on disabled children's language development with a caregiver who asked about this and expressed concerns.

COMMUNICATIVE JUSTICE TAKEAWAYS

At a certain point in a research project, you realize that you could analyze the data in new, different, and fascinating ways forever. When this realization hits, academics often offer the adage, "Just get it done." But when you're doing the research with and for a community whom you love deeply, "Just get it done" feels like a small violence. This begs the question of who the book is for. On the one hand, it is for schools and practitioners. It is for educators to learn how to better listen to and uplift the expertise of these young children and their families. It is for the institution of schooling, to reorient toward learning that addresses the whole child and their communities of communication. This is for these young children and families. This disruption is for them. This publication is for them, in the hopes that our systems start to shift, that educators assume shared responsibility and comprehension of communicative justice, that families need to expend less labor teaching teachers how to teach their children.

Our (emergent) bilingual young people who communicate outside of spoken named languages are making new paths for others who walk and speak differently, or who move and communicate differently, since not everyone walks and speaks in the traditional senses of the words. As García (2019) so beautifully words it,

> 'No hay camino' [there is no path], as the Spanish poet, Antonio Machado tells us. Instead, 'se hace camino al andar' [You make the road by walking] . . . translanguaging can set a new path, one that can only be found as we walk towards an educational system that is not simply a continued mechanism of coloniality, but that makes new paths for others who walk and speak differently. (p. 372)

Educational professionals and learning spaces are often positioned as bastions of change, innovation, and expertise. In reality, the change is already happening within the families and communities where our students live, learn, grow, and communicate. They are engaged in this dance, building these pathways for expressing and understanding. The school, in this book, becomes the listening subject alongside myself as researcher. How must our listening gaze/stance shift to attend to this dance that is happening beyond school walls? How do parents/caregivers understand the communication practices of their nonspeaking bilingual children? How do bilingual nonspeaking children express themselves, both to new people (i.e., myself as the researcher) and to their family members (i.e., what I noticed via family visits/observations)? May this work open new caminos for us all to move and communicate more fully with one another—for nonspeaking bilingual children, but also for all children and educators to learn new pathways of communicating and being in community with one another. Ultimately this book is built on the premise that children and families deserve systems that are built for them, not systems that accommodate them as an afterthought, or not at all, and teachers deserve better preparation and support in being the co-learners all children deserve.

OVERVIEW OF CHAPTERS

Each chapter will be structured with the following sections to help illuminate and invite us toward communicative justice in our classrooms and lives: Key Idea(s); The Status Quo: Problematic Current Practices; Learnings from Children, Families, and Educators; Communicative Justice Takeaways; and Teaching in Action. The Key Idea(s) will introduce the heart of the chapter and the ideas that are being offered; The Status Quo: Problematic Current Practices section identifies the ideologies and practices that currently exist that we need to reimagine and challenge; Learnings from Children, Families, and Educators introduces quotes and experiences from nonspeaking bilingual children, their families, and their educators to center the narratives of those most intimate with these issues; Communicative Justice Takeaways summarize the previous sections into learnings we can implement in our classrooms; and the Teaching in Action section at the end of each chapter provides tangible resources for implementing and deepening communicative justice in your own classroom or learning environment.

Chapter 1 introduces the reader to the focal participants—the children—from the case studies that are centered in the book. It explains why centering the communication practices of bi/multilingual nonspeaking children can lead to more compassionate and comprehensive communication practices for all of us—adults and children alike. This chapter builds on the concept that "None of us is free until all of us are free," and presents the framework of multimodal and multilingual expression and engagement in learning spaces as a transformative benefit to all learners. Included in this chapter are action steps for educators to examine where their schools and practices fall within culturally responsive-sustaining and disability justice frameworks, and how to begin to deepen their justice-oriented pedagogy.

Chapter 2 identifies current theories of languaging and/or pedagogy that offer openings for expanding our conceptions of languaging and literacy to nonspeaking communication. It provides context for the current and historical state of schooling for multilingual nonspeaking children—bilingual and special education programming, related services, and programming available in general education settings. It introduces the research study that led to this book and the theories that undergird the analysis of the case studies of the families in the study. This chapter includes "Teaching in Action" to ensure that educators, children, and families have an open dialogue about the policies, programs, rights, and ideological stances involved in the education of the nonspeaking multilingual child.

Chapter 3 addresses the persistent myth that bilingualism is too confusing for children with disabilities. It presents research to dispel this misconception and highlights examples from my research and case studies to identify practices of multilingual, multimodal literacies that are often disregarded in formal educational spaces. It also highlights how families of bilingual nonspeaking children experience this confusing narrative when navigating the school system with their children. It examines the exhausting trope that any deviance from a mythical neurotypical, monolingual English-speaking, white, middle-class child requires hegemonic monolingual English instruction. This chapter includes "Teaching in Action" for educators to support families in finding and selecting the best program for their child, and also in making their own classrooms or learning environments more geared toward multilingualism and multimodal practices.

Chapter 4 highlights unique familial communication systems of bilingual nonspeaking children and their families. This includes gesture-based communication, guessing games that parents created to ease their child's frustration and ensure full understanding, and the ways that parents and caregivers identified the strengths, needs, and experiences of their children in ways that medical and educational professionals could not or did not. This chapter introduces a theory of "reciprocal carryover," uplifting case studies of families communicating beyond the spoken word, with action steps for how educators can learn from children and families to carry over communicative practices into formal educational spaces; the chapter concludes with "Teaching in Action" for educators to learn about these systems from children and families that they work with.

Chapter 5 explores the notion of "intent to communicate," drawing on an educator interview wherein the speech language pathologist asserted that one nonspeaking bilingual child had "no intent" to communicate. This chapter examines the perceiving and expressing subject, communication partnerships, and the (mis)understandings that happen between nonspeaking bilingual children, their families, and their educators.

The conclusion synthesizes what I hope the reader has learned about languaging, communication practices, and the relationships between home and school for these nonspeaking bilingual children and their families. This chapter provides an overview of the tools, strategies, and lessons from the book, and turns toward hopeful futures of liberatory languaging.

This introduction opened with a quote from Arundhati Roy: "Another world is not only possible, she is on her way. On a quiet day, I can hear her breathing." This book invites us all to consider: What can we "hear" in our classrooms when we respect and honor the children who live in the "quiet"?

TEACHING IN ACTION

More Than Words in the Classroom

As mentioned in the chapter descriptions, each chapter will offer "Teaching in Action" sections to connect the chapter content to applied classroom practice. I begin with offering a companion activity to a read-aloud that centers expansive communication and communicative justice in a beautiful, kid-friendly way. May we always remember that this work is not just intellectual and theoretical but matters most when we put it into action with our young people to build a better world together with and for them.

The children's book *More Than Words: So Many Ways to Say What We Mean,* by Roz MacLean (2023), focuses on a young boy who does not use spoken language as his primary form of expression. The book walks children through all the various ways that we express ourselves, even if we also are people who use spoken words. It shows examples like facial expression, body movements, and sign language.

Question(s) for Students: The book concludes with ***asking children to consider*** what are ways that you might know that your classmate is trying to be your friend that don't use spoken words? *You can build on this to ask your students to reflect:* How do you share your ideas and feelings with your friends? On the playground? (Prompt: When you play games like tag, how do you communicate? ***Potential answers might include:*** *We use our bodies, we wave to signal at each other, we laugh a lot.)*

Question(s) for Students: How might you know that someone is trying to communicate with you or be your friend during morning meeting? (Prompt: What activities do we do in morning meeting?

> How do you share with your classmates and friends during these activities? *Examples might include singing together, dancing together, passing an object around to indicate whose turn is next, and so on).*

Make sure to include multimodal options for children to engage and respond, such as drawing their responses; selecting drawn pictures or photographs from an array of options; writing; using an AAC (alternative and augmentative communication) device; using visual boards; acting out their responses with their bodies, puppets, and/or words; and providing spoken responses. Helping students identify all the ways that they use nonvocal or nonverbal communication with one another, even if they also use spoken words, can help set the tone for normalizing a shared, working definition of communication that goes beyond spoken language to honor the myriad ways we as humans connect with one another.

CHAPTER 1

None of Us Is Free Until All of Us Are Free

> If you have come here to help me, you are wasting your time. But if you have come because your liberation is bound up with mine, then let us work together.
>
> —Aboriginal saying, often attributed to visual artist Lilla Watson

"LISTENING" TO ALL FORMS OF "SPEAKING"

In my early years of classroom teaching, I had a student, Veronica, who was classified as minimally verbal. Our classroom was a monolingual English special education room on paper, but in reality, most of the students were bilingual. Veronica repeated some words in both Spanish and English when they were spoken to her and would sometimes say one or two words at a time, but the majority of the time, she did not use spoken words to communicate. I will never forget the day that I came to school with a sprained ankle, wrapped in a bandage underneath a leg brace. I had doctor's orders to keep my foot elevated at all times, and truth be told, I probably shouldn't have been teaching at all that day. But I was an early career public school teacher and did not have the sick days in my bank to be able to take multiple days off to elevate my leg, so I found myself trekking 2 hours on the New York City subway to get to work to teach my class of 3rd- to 5th-graders in a self-contained special education classroom. My student Veronica would spend the better part of an hour erasing and rewriting her letters to make them as perfect as possible. In an effort to get her to finish her Daily Journal entry, I sat next to her and stopped her from erasing her already-formed letters that were perfectly legible. She glared at me. I knew from that glare that she was not happy, but she complied, writing her response to the morning prompt without erasing her letters or words. I was satisfied with myself that I had supported her in working through a compulsion, completing the assigned task, and meeting the morning's objective.

Later that day, after lunch, we were doing a math lesson on multiplication. As I sat at the front of the room modeling a multiplication problem on the board, Veronica got up to sharpen her pencil. As she neared the front of the room, I recognized the same glare she had cast my way when we were doing Morning Journals. She quickly walked past me toward the sharpener, looking me in my eyes, looking down at my elevated ankle propped up on the chair next to me, and then quickly brought her fist down on my ankle. My eyes filled with tears from the pain, but also from the recognition that my student had found a way to communicate her dissent and discontent from earlier that day. Of course, violence is not the type of communication we encourage, but this moment revealed to me just how oppressive my own communication practices were. I knew that my student was extremely unhappy when she was not allowed to erase and rewrite her letters, and I did not create any space for that discussion. Because she did not use spoken words, I steamrolled her thoughts and feelings and imposed my own. She had clearly been observing me all day and was aware of what was happening with my leg. She had also figured out how to indicate her unhappiness with me. Again, I am not saying this to praise the choice she made to inflict pain, but to acknowledge that if we do not create systems in our classrooms for our nonspeaking students to share their ideas, desires, and needs with us, they will find their own ways. When students are nonspeaking and also bilingual, their communication is often discounted in multiple ways; in addition to not honoring their "voice," we often place them in monolingual English special education classrooms, like the one that I taught that year. Communication always finds a way; whether or not we pay attention is another matter. The pain in my ankle led me to the realization that something had to change in the way that I approached communication in my classroom. My student was telling me, very plainly, that she would not be ignored. She was an active member of the classroom community, and I had not been respecting her and her voice in the ways she deserved.

KEY IDEA(S)

Centering the communication practices of multilingual nonspeaking children can lead to more compassionate and comprehensive communication practices for all of us—adults and children alike. While liberation is often used as an abstract buzzword in educational discourse, I begin to form a concrete picture of what this means in regard to communicative justice by uplifting the notion popularized by activists like Fannie Lou Hamer and Emma Lazarus that *nobody is free until everyone is free.* In learning spaces, this means that we must expand our understanding of communication to include not only multilingual spoken communication, but additional modalities of expression like gesture, body movements, facial expressions, and eye gaze as well. Expanding what we perceive as "legitimate" and legible communication can benefit all learners. Even children who *do* speak to communicate may also express themselves with gestures and physical movement that often goes unperceived in classrooms. One example I always think of when it comes to gesture is pointing. Pointing is a gesture, so as educators, we may think that allowing children to point with their finger(s) as a form of expression means we are engaging in multimodal communication with our students. However, in many cultures, people point with their mouth and/or chin to indicate where something is. If a child points using their face—their mouth or chin—rather than their finger, and a teacher is not culturally equipped to recognize this gesture, then this gesture goes unperceived and the child's knowledge and expression goes unrecognized by their teacher. This culturally responsive, sustaining layer to multimodal communication impacts nonspeaking bilingual children, of course, but also impacts all children and teachers as they navigate communication across and within multiple cultures. The way that someone points (i.e., with their hand or with their mouth) is a form of multilingual, unspoken communication. As classroom teachers, we often are not trained to recognize that multilingualism can be nonverbal. Until we have communication systems, knowledge, and structures in place to support multiple forms of communication, we will miss so much of what our children have to share—like I missed out on learning from and with my student before she decided to get my attention via my sprained ankle. In a classroom focused on expansive communication, every individual can be understood by their audience in a way that aligns as much as possible with the meaning the individual intended to communicate. Without these expansive understandings of communication, we cannot consider our classrooms spaces of true learning—or liberation.

Recently, as I was serving on a planning committee for a major conference, we were reviewing many applications that used the jargon and terminology of the conference theme on social justice, but the meat of these proposals and projects was not rooted in or oriented toward justice. When we met to discuss the submissions, we all agreed: People had used key words to "accessorize" their submissions. This accessorizing of our work is an attractive pitfall in academia, but at what cost? Using certain words feels fancy and important—and words are certainly important and powerful. In the section that follows, I will explain the terms *raciolinguistics* and a *racioliguistic perspective*. The use of these terms signifies at least peripheral interaction with higher education and academia. But the concepts themselves are not so inaccessible when we break them down. What is it that makes us feel the need to explain something in a way that requires multiple years of advanced schooling to understand? I think a lot about the difference between schooling and education. The president of the university where I teach, Dr. Mariana Souto-Manning, once said, "I am highly schooled, which is different from being highly educated." This rings true for me: I am highly schooled, which is different from being highly educated. The stories of children and families in this book continue to educate me beyond anything I could possibly learn in a university classroom.

I write this as an offering to all the brilliant members of my community who deserve books like this that don't create barriers between the concepts and the community. In a graduate course that I taught years ago at Hunter College in New York, a bilingual special education teacher candidate slammed her copy of a popularly assigned book on equity on the desk in frustration and turned to me, saying: "This text is *not* meeting my access needs." She said the constant in-text citations in parentheses made it nearly impossible for her to read the sentences, let alone apply the material in a way that was meaningful for her students in her elementary classroom. In the same ways that I propose we expand our communication systems to nurture and sustain communication communities with young children in our classrooms, I propose that those of us in academia expand our communication systems to express ourselves in ways that make sense to the people we need to learn from, and open our frameworks for how we understand the communication of those we need to "listen" to the most: our families, our communities, and our children. Finally, I offer that education research in academia only matters if it is useful for educators on the ground. This may seem to be common sense, but you would be surprised at how much academic writing and research is inaccessible for teachers. As a former public school teacher myself, my commitment is to children, families, communities, and the educators who teach and love them every day.

THE STATUS QUO: PROBLEMATIC CURRENT PRACTICES

Communication is impacted and influenced by our own racial identities and racial biases (Flores & Rosa, 2015). A raciolinguistic perspective helps us understand that there are certain ways of using language that are considered good, valuable, and/or appropriate, especially in schooling. When students use language that does not fit this "academic" standard, they are labeled as deficient; as lesser; as not as appropriate, valuable, or capable. For students who are Black and Brown, this is especially relevant. They are automatically viewed as having lesser language skills; the way a Mexican student labeled as an English learner is viewed for having an accent in school is very different from the way a French student is viewed in U.S. schools, for example.

A tweet by the *Daily Mirror* (2018) helps outline the ways that this dynamic plays out. The *Daily Mirror* wrote, "Princess Charlotte already speaks two languages at just two years old," sharing a photo of the United

Kingdom's toddler Princess Charlotte. As evidenced in this *Daily Mirror* post, the Internet went wild for Princess Charlotte speaking two languages at such a young age, regarding it as extremely impressive. X (formerly Twitter) user cole responded, "so do most children of immigrants but I guess it's less impressive when they're poor" (@_colenewberry, 2018). What this tweet misses is that there is also a racial component intertwined with class and language here. A raciolinguistic perspective helps us understand the idea that Black, Brown, and other children who are not white are viewed as "behind" because of their multilingualism, while white children are viewed as exceptional for theirs. Flores & Rosa (2015) write about the idea of the racialized subject, meaning a student or child who is not white. In academia, we often use the word *racialized* to recognize that race is a social construct and so people of color have been labeled with their "race" and subjugated because of it. The system of power and hierarchy that we experience because of race is not natural; we have been racialized by human-constructed ideas and social structures.

The racialized subject is the student or young person who is viewed as lesser for the way that they speak. The person viewing and labeling them as lesser is the white listening subject. We can think about the white listening subject as the teacher in this example. Even if the teacher is not a white person, the power dynamic of them labeling a racialized kid as deficient makes them a white listening subject because they are telling the kid that their ways of speaking and expressing themselves are wrong if/when they don't exactly line up with the "academic" standards of language at school. Because these academic standards of language are so often rooted in white, upper-middle-class norms of speaking, writing, and communicating, a teacher who insists that children must speak in this way to be "correct" is upholding a white view of the children. This is why the teacher is the white listening subject in this framework; they are protecting and imposing white standards of communicating, and they only "hear" children as valuable or correct when they speak/communicate according to those standards and rules of language. Anything outside of that, they label as wrong and in need of fixing.

I propose that we think about communication beyond just a speaking and listening subject. We need to think beyond how kids "talk" and how teachers "listen." We need to think about talking as more than vocal speech and listening as more than auditory input. As we saw in the opening anecdote about Veronica, she was communicating using facial expressions, gestures, and physical movements. I initially failed to "listen" to her expression because it was not shared in spoken form. We need to think about how children communicate in full, expansive ways, and how teachers perceive them. María Cioè-Peña (2021a) has taken the idea of the white listening subject from raciolinguistics and pushed on the idea to include the white *perceiving* subject. How do we perceive our children, and how do we fail at perceiving their communication, in ways that move beyond listening to spoken language? We need to be better perceptive partners, better communication partners, with our students. When a kid is doing something that seems like a tantrum, what are they communicating to us? As educators, we must identify the areas where we need to adjust our understandings and systems to ensure that we are honoring the full identities and communicative practices of our racialized young people, our multilingual young people, our disabled young people, our young people living at all these intersections. We must identify the ways that we are currently marking these children as deficient, as "other," as having "bad" language habits or skills, as using language in ways that don't belong in school. I invite us to ask instead, *how can we fix or transform schools to be spaces where all communication and language use is heard, perceived, understood, and valued?*

As social media permeates our lives, we find ourselves with increasing access to different viewpoints and ways of thinking. More and more, the notion of questioning our own communicative capabilities and skills, rather than just those of our children/students, has been taken up in public discourse. TikTok and Instagram posts often call for transformative turns that reach the public in ways that academic articles and theories often do not. One Instagram post in particular, by The Informed SLP (2023), talked about misaligned communication modes/styles from a speech language pathology perspective.

> *Slide 1:* Understanding another neurotype's social interactions is *not* just the responsibility of autistic people.
>
> *Slide 2:* Non-autistic individuals have communicative difficulties when interacting with autistic individuals (Crompton et al., 2020).
>
> *Slide 3:* What we've been calling *deficits* in social communication may actually be a *mismatch* in communicative styles (The Informed SLP, 2023).

The expansion of these theories beyond the conceptual academic realm into the hands (and handles) of educators, caregivers, and the public in general helps us all, as a collective, turn the lens on the perceiving subject/educator/professional to expand our skills as well as how we recognize and perceive communication.

When I was looking for a home for this book, I spoke with one well-known, more commercial publishing house who told me that centering bilingual nonspeaking students was too narrow a focus for a mostly general education teacher audience and did not have "market pull." The notion that relearning our understandings of and approaches to communication only applies to special education teachers, or bilingual education teachers, or bilingual special education teachers, suggests that the way communication happens right now in classrooms works for all children. I suggest that the way classroom communication occurs currently does not work for most children. Policies that enforce "standard academic English," or white mainstream spoken English (WMSE) as the only acceptable form of languaging appear in classrooms across the United States—and that is just the tip of the iceberg with the policing of spoken language. In 2024, a list of "Prohibited Classroom Words" went viral on X (formerly known as Twitter). This list included words and phrases like "bruh," "cap," "standing on business," and "period!" and the accompanying note said that anyone "caught" using these words would be required to write a short essay explaining why those chose to use said words. The note from the teacher also said that "slang" is not an appropriate way to express oneself in an academic setting (@backendzyy, 2024). This list and note are an example of language policing that happens in classrooms.

Rewiring how we communicate, how we listen, and how we perceive is a task that benefits all children and ourselves. It opens the door for us to fully understand and see one another beyond the confines of spoken standardized English. In her book *More-Than-Human Literacies in Early Childhood*, Abigail Hackett (2021) addresses the notion that exceptionalizing certain identities and forms of expression is part of the problem. Instead, we should think of [nonspeaking bilingual] children and their practices as ordinary. "The lives of young children and their parents in these communities are ordinary. . . . This ordinariness is the starting point if we are to begin to understand young children's literacy and language practices" (Hackett, 2021, p. 7). The notion of ordinariness is important, to reorient toward our nonspeaking, multilingual children and their families as ordinary, rather than anomalies in need of "exceptional" and "special" labels and treatment.

I met a principal recently who had paid money out of her own pocket to get large visual communication boards installed all over the school playground. She was working to train all staff and students in how to use communication boards to communicate, so the nonspeaking children were not the only ones utilizing these visual aids on the playground. The goal was for all students to use the visual communication boards as one of their many tools to communicate with one another. Imagine if we had multilingual visual communication boards that had both pictures and multilingual words labeling the pictures on every playground, and if every student and teacher were trained in how to use them! This principal modeled an understanding that the use of visual aids can and should be ordinary, not just for nonspeaking children, but for all people who communicate. Situating communication tools like this as ordinary helps us expand our notions of and need for communicative justice and expansive communication for all teachers and learners. Centering the idea that "None of us is free until all of us are free" helps us understand that *none* of us has communicative justice until *all* of us have communicative justice. Michelle Salazar Pérez, in a chapter in *Black Feminist Thought in Early Childhood Studies* (2017), wrote that many people have questioned her, asking, "'how is *this* early childhood?'" (p. 51). Similarly, I have gotten the question about my work: "How is *this* for all educators and children?" That is what this chapter, and I hope this book, will answer.

LEARNINGS FROM CHILDREN, FAMILIES, AND EDUCATORS

The examples in this book come from five families I had the deep honor of working with and learning from. Each family self-identified into the study by indicating that a nonspeaking, nonverbal, or minimally verbal bilingual child was a member of their family.

Niveyah

When Niveyah, a 4-year-old nonspeaking bilingual child, wanted her sisters' attention, she would make a sound between a yell and a grunt to secure their attention, and then either point or physically run toward another area, and the sisters would follow. Niveyah's mother described her as an extremely bright child who understands both Spanish and English. She proudly described her aptitude in math counting and alphabet games that she plays in both languages on her tablet. She had not sent her to school yet because she was still young enough to stay home, and her mother was worried about her being bullied at school because she did not speak to communicate and did not yet use the toilet independently.

Hector

Hector, a 3-year-old boy whose mother identified him as minimally verbal and previously nonverbal, repeated a lot of the words and sentences that I asked him during our interview, and at times said things that seemed outside the bounds of the explicitness that I was seeking with my questions. For example, he made a comment that he was mad at school and broke a tower. I asked if he did it on accident or on purpose, and he replied, "I just do it on purpose on accident." His mother expressed concern that things like this happened at school and she was unable to figure out what happened from his spoken language; she had to rely on teachers to communicate with her, and in her experience she found that the teachers didn't attend to his communication in a holistic way.

Bernardo

Bernardo, a 3-year-old boy; his mother; and I spent time together on Zoom—one of the many side effects of the pandemic. Interestingly, despite his parents only speaking to him in Spanish, when I asked him a question that he did not seem to understand, in both English and Spanish, he turned to his mom and said, "Hmm? What she say, mama?" and she would repeat my question in Spanish. Bernardo's teachers used only English with him, since his school did not have staff who spoke Spanish and did not offer bilingual programming. When his mother signed up to participate in the project, she shared that she felt Bernardo was minimally verbal and his language seemed delayed to her; she was worried that there might be an issue, and she was not sure how connected it was or was not to his bilingualism.

Emmanual

Emmanual, a 9-year-old boy who did not use spoken words at all to communicate until he was 5 years old and spent his pre-K–3rd-grade years in self-contained special education classrooms, told me that he only spoke English. However, his mother shared that when she, her husband, and Emmanual's older brother were conversing in Spanish, Emmanual would ask follow-up questions that indicated he comprehended the Spanish languaging that occurred. Emmanual and his mother were offered only English language special education services and programs, despite the family's bilingualism and the fact that Emmanual's grandparents only spoke Spanish. His mother, a bilingual teacher herself, shared that she was worried that using both languages with him would confuse him.

Katrina

Katrina was a 3-year-old girl whose mother identified her as nonverbal. Her mom and her bilingual speech-language pathologist both gave interviews, but as Katrina began speaking more, her mom opted not to continue with the child interview and family observation aspect of the study. Her speech-language pathologist described her language as a growth spurt, likening it to a tree's progression. Both mom and the speech-language pathologist indicated that Katrina had no dominant language and would express herself and respond to both English and Spanish, though she tended to use Spanish for food more than anything.

COMMUNICATIVE JUSTICE TAKEAWAYS

U.S. schools push the idea that speaking "standard academic English" is the ultimate goal for academic achievement. Teachers and service providers are held to state and national standards that equate success with development of spoken English. If we push a little deeper, we uncover that using spoken language is considered a marker of what makes us human and what distinguishes us from other animals and species. This connection between spoken language and humanness is one that carries significant weight for children who are multiply marginalized, by virtue of being both nonspeaking and multilingual (and, of course, often non-white). This ideology also works to dehumanize disabled people who do not speak to communicate.

Melanie Yergeau writes in *Authoring Autism* (2018) that she used to wet herself at school, and that her mom would find her in her crib up to her neck in feces when she was little. This was all setting the stage to describe her childhood pre-diagnosis for autism. At least two of the moms whose families are centered in this book discuss potty training and their fear of their child not being able to use the bathroom. Yergeau says,

> I very clearly remember the long process of being toilet trained. . . . By contrast, I do not remember learning to read. Decoding symbols felt less effortful, even as a toddler, but decoding my body—decoding sensations, recognizing which tightness meant which function, rehearsing the order of bodily motions required to use a toilet—these things long eluded me . . . (2018, p. 6).

What would it mean for us to help children learn to decode their own bodies, and in turn for us to learn from them about their bodily movements and what they intend to express? Goldin-Meadow (2015) writes about gestural development in young children becoming more advanced as children are able to use gesture with intent. *When children do not communicate with spoken language, when they are often not understood clearly by their teachers and adults in their lives, how do we work to understand their physical movements? How do we ensure we are not projecting our own interpretations onto children, but are actually committed to perceiving what children are telling us?*

When I was a special education teacher, I was advised to "extinguish" certain physical movements that my students engaged in, like "stimming," which often included rocking back and forth, flapping their arms or hands, and sometimes spinning in circles or knocking their heads against a wall. While knocking a head against a wall is something that can harm a child, the other physical movements do not harm the child or anyone else in the classroom. If rocking back and forth soothes a child's mind and eases their sensory overload, why would we identify that as a "wrong" or "bad" action? Becoming better communication partners with our students means considering that movements like flapping your hands might be communicating something to us. Perhaps a child is on sensory overload and the movement is helping them self-regulate. Perhaps it just feels good to them. Our work as educators, and as human beings in community in this world, should not be to hold children to a "normal" marker of behavior. If the behaviors are not harming the child or anyone around them, who are we to label them as wrong? Our work is to open ourselves up to listening, perceiving, learning, and nurturing our students based on the myriad ways they communicate to us.

Teacher preparation programs today are largely oriented away from the once-pervasive narrative of "giving voice to the voiceless." We are in an era where many people recognize that everyone has a voice, but some have been deliberately and systematically silenced or unheard. This rewriting of the narrative, though powerful, still often marginalizes students who have historically been some of the most vulnerable. *For nonspeaking students who do not vocalize their speech to communicate, what does honoring and attending to their voice look and sound like?* We will explore the many different ways that children express their "voice" throughout this book. I encourage you to begin reflecting on how you understand your students' voices in unspoken ways.

In the same way that many early childhood and childhood educators can make meaning of inventive spelling as children are learning to write, so can many caregivers make sense of the inventive language that children use—both spoken and unspoken. One mom in the study, Florence, mentioned knowing what her son Bernardo meant when he said something that no one else would necessarily understand. She said,

> He mixes English and Spanish together and sometimes, like if you don't know him, you won't know what he's saying. So for example the other day, he really has this thing now where he wants to take off his own shoes, um, like he gets really upset if I take them off now, and so the other day we came home, and like, um, I forgot that he had this thing now and accidentally took off his shoes, and he got really upset and he goes, "I love it patos, I love it patos!" Um, which I knew like meant, like I like to take off my shoes, 'cause zapatos is shoes in Spanish and . . . And he usually just says I love it anytime that he wants to say he likes something, and so I had to put his shoes back on, and let him take them off. But like nobody else would know that "I love it patos!" means that he wants to take off his shoes.

Because Bernardo's expression was starting to mirror what is more typically understood in terms of vocal expression in both English and Spanish, this type of expression might be easier for us as educators to perceive. Using the tools that caregivers and educators already have to make sense of children's expressions of frustration and desire can help us to expand our perceptive skills even further, to learn to read and react to communication from children who do not use spoken words.

Culturally responsive-sustaining multimodal communication impacts not just nonspeaking bilingual children, but all children and teachers as they navigate communication across and within multiple cultures. Until we have communication systems, knowledges, and structures in place to support a communication community—that is, every party can be understood/perceived by their intended audience in reasonable alignment with their intended meaning—we cannot consider our classrooms spaces of true learning—or liberation.

TEACHING IN ACTION

As we move toward analyzing our learning environments and how we create space for and attend to various student "voices," it is important to involve students in evaluating their own learning progress. Students are so often left out of the conversations around their learning, and are particularly excluded from conversations related to their IEPs. Working toward freedom of expression and communication in our classrooms is not solely confined to what modes of communication we use (i.e., spoken words, written words, drawings, gestures, facial expressions); creating learning environments where everyone is free to express themselves requires us to honor and acknowledge all aspects of our students' identities. For our bilingual nonspeaking students, this means explicitly discussing the learning strategies, supports, accommodations, and goals that are written for them. It also means collaborating with them to determine which of those feel useful to them.

In Table 1.1, I offer a tool I developed called SIP: Student-driven Individualized Education Program Practice (Padía, 2024). This tool was designed to help students self-monitor and share their feelings about their progress toward their academic goals, as well as to identify tools that helped them work toward their goals. I have adapted the SIP tool to focus on communication in what I call SAC: Student Agency in Communication (Table 1.2). Finally, I present a Communicative Justice in Action (CJA) Planning Tool for educators (Table 1.3). Based on what you learn from implementing the SIP and SAC protocols with students, you can use the CJA Planning Tool to analyze your lessons and learning environment and adjust it to meet the strengths and needs of all your students—particularly those who are bilingual and nonspeaking, who so rarely are given the opportunity to provide input on their own learning experience. The most important thing to keep at the center of our work here is that we should not be talking *about* our students, their communication, and their learning, but talking *with* them. They are, after all, the experts of their own learning and expression. When we are planning our lessons, activities, and assessments, we must center how our students will engage, how we will show up as communication partners,

Table 1.1. SIP (Student-driven IEP Practice) in Action Protocol

1. Print the Annual Goals of a student's IEP and/or pull it up on a tablet or accessible device.
2. Review the Annual Goals and together select/highlight the one(s) that align to Language Arts overall.
3. Looking at the Learning Objective and the class activities for the day for ELA, identify which Annual Goal best aligns and have the student record both the Learning Objective and the aligned Annual Goal.
4. Have students identify their accommodations that might be relevant for this lesson.
5. Work together to identify what the student will demonstrate tied to their Annual Goal. (For example, if the goal is "Will write a full paragraph with introductory sentence, body sentences, and conclusion sentence," the "Will" for the day might be "write a complete sentence.")
6. At the end of the lesson, have students self-assess. These data can help students get a clear picture as time wears on of their progress toward their goals, the class objectives, and an understanding of which accommodations support their learning and in what ways. (Bonus: It also provides you with data to justify their IEP progress when you have to complete Progress Monitoring Reports!)

Note: Consider having a self-assessment for *all* of your students, as this is a crucial part of reflecting on learning for all learners, and doing this collectively also reinforces the destigmatization of using and assessing individual progress on a regular basis.

and what steps we can take to foster true, holistic communication within our classrooms.

When I was a classroom teacher, I would routinely use SIP and SAC protocols with my students. I was amazed at how often students had no idea what accommodations they were entitled to. I was also shocked to see how rarely they would identify the accommodations on their IEPs as helpful. One nonspeaking bilingual student of mine had an IEP accommodation that said he would always have access to a bilingual Spanish-English visual board on his desk. However, because IEPs are typically only updated once a year, his IEP was out of date; this student had received a bilingually programmed AAC device since the IEP was written, and since receiving the device, had completely stopped relying on the laminated visual board that was taped to his desk. As his teacher, it was my job to work with the speech language therapist and the special education coordinator to update and amend his IEP. Had I not gone through the SIP and SAC protocols with him, I would not have realized how out of date the IEP was. Our students should always be in the driver's seat of their own learning whenever possible. We are there to support them and empower them to take the wheel. Our nonspeaking bilingual students are so rarely given this opportunity. This should not be an

Table 1.2. SAC: Student Agency in Communication

SAC: Student Agency in Communication (SIP Protocol adapted for Communicative Justice)
1. If a student has an IEP, print the IEP or pull it up on a tablet or screen to review together. Identify places where it says the student will communicate and how they communicate. Consider: Do they use a device? What spoken languages does it say they use? What is the language and/or modality of instruction that is identified for their learning?
2. Whether or not a student has an IEP, identify together how they prefer to communicate. Ask them to identify all the ways that they like to receive information: written words, photographs, videos, drawings, music/songs, auditory recordings, gestures, and any others that you might think of. Students can indicate this by selecting items on a device, writing, drawing, speaking, or using their bodies to indicate which they prefer. Then ask them to identify all the ways they like to share information: written words, photographs, videos, drawings, music/songs, auditory recordings, gestures, and any others that you might think of. Students can indicate this by selecting items on a device, writing, drawing, speaking, or using their bodies to indicate which they prefer. It is important to share with them that this is a living document that you all will update together on a regular basis, so if they find a modality that really works for them in the future, you will update this list together.
3. Looking at the Learning Objective and the class activities for the day, identify which modalities you as the educator have designed/provided for the child to engage with the activity/ies.
4. Together with the student, identify the options they will have for accessing information and the different opportunities they will have to express themselves, both to you as the educator and to their peers within the activity/ies.
5. At the end of the lesson, have students reflect on the lesson. How did they learn during this activity? How did they express themselves during this activity? Some students will just identify the modality (i.e., did we watch a video, did we sing a song, did we look at photographs?) while other students may be more advanced and will identify all the modalities used and then which they preferred.

Note: Consider this communication assessment process for *all* of your students, as this is a crucial part of reflecting on learning for all learners, and doing this collectively also reinforces the destigmatization of using and assessing individual progress on a regular basis. It also reinforces the notion that expansive communication is something that everyone engages in and everyone can benefit from; gestures, videos, audio, and graphics are practices that work for many of us, regardless of whether or not we also speak to communicate.

Table 1.3. Communicative Justice in Action (CJA) Planning Tool

Daily Learning Objective	Learning Activities	Types of Materials and Resources	Opportunities for Communication	Documentation
Today we will . . . *(indicate the skill the students will learn/ demonstrate)*	*(List what students will be engaged in that day; e.g., creating a collage, writing a paragraph, sorting and matching, etc.)*	*(List all resources and modalities here; e.g., visuals on a smartboard, manipulatives for students to move around on their desk, visual boards for students to respond to questions, etc. For some students, it may be helpful to use photos or visuals of the different options, like a photo of headphones for audiobook options, a photo of the smartboard for interactive lessons, etc.)*	*(List all modes of expression that will be included in the activity; e.g., AAC devices, pointing, drawing, writing, speaking, body movement/role play, use of puppets, etc. Identify which modes will be available during which learning activities.)*	*(List how you will document the learning and expression of the student(s). Will you record the interactions to capture gestures? Will you or a colleague take anecdotal notes? Will you take photographs of students' responses?)*

exceptional practice. Our role as educators is to make this type of student ownership ordinary for all our learners.

PLANNING FOR COMMUNICATIVE JUSTICE IN YOUR DAILY LESSONS

The CJA tool is for educators to use for lesson and activity planning after engaging in SIP and SAC protocols with students. SIP and SAC are not intended to be used just once with each student, but on an ongoing basis. The results of the SIP and SAC should inform our lesson planning and reflection as educators. The CJA tool can help us incorporate what we learn about and from our students to make our learning environments and activities as accessible and inclusive as possible. For the student I listed above who no longer used the bilingual communication board listed on his IEP, I started incorporating his communication device into my planning. Sometimes this would require that I preload his AAC device with certain vocabulary words in both Spanish and English for the lessons of the week. Other times it meant I would set up Think-Pair-Share activities to plan for a speaking student to exchange questions and answers with the student who used the device, so I would program the device with the questions that were on the class worksheets. Honoring our students as drivers in the learning process means using their input to inform our own planning as educators. Rather than deciding what is best for our students, we can use the SIP, SAC, and CJA to decide on best practices together *with* our students.

CHAPTER 2

Expansive Theories of Communication

> The problem is, some of y'all are trying to sit at tables God sent you to flip.
>
> —Camille Walker

COMMUNICATION REQUIRES COLLECTIVE COMMITMENT

When I was an instructional coach in the Bronx, New York, I supported teachers and classrooms grades Pre-K through 8. One of the 7th-grade students in our school was both nonspeaking and bilingual. He was labeled as an English Language Learner by the school system because his family was from a country that spoke French, though he was not in a bilingual class because we only offered Spanish-English bilingual classes at our school—and even those were small in number and not offered for every grade. This particular student, who we will call Nasir, was a Black boy who at age 11 was already almost 6 feet tall. He had been with us in the school for several years, since he was much younger and much smaller in size. It was well known throughout the school that Nasir loved coffee; teachers and paraprofessionals would laugh affectionately and remind each other to hide their coffee cups up out of Nasir's reach, lest they turn their backs for a moment and find him slurping down their caffeine.

One Monday morning, Nasir's mom showed up extremely distraught as she dropped him off at school. She informed us that over the weekend, the two of them had been walking outside. They stopped near a coffee truck, and she was distracted for a moment. When she looked for Nasir to continue their walk, she was horrified to find him pinned to the ground. In the moments she had turned away, he followed the scent of coffee, his familiar favorite, and jumped into the back of the coffee truck. A police officer happened to be nearby and tackled him to the ground, attempting to place handcuffs on him. Though his mom was not fully comfortable or confident in English, she spoke enough to explain to the officer and coffee cart owner that her son had autism and was still a child. Still, she shared with us that following Monday morning at school that it took her a while to get her words out in English. They let him go, but not every child is so lucky.

I was teaching 3rd- to 5th-grade students with autism the year that Tamir Rice, a 12-year-old Black boy, was shot and killed for playing on a public playground, because onlookers and police both wrongly assumed that he had a working firearm. For our students who are both nonspeaking and bilingual, whose families might not use English to communicate with law enforcement or other people and institutions of power, the stakes are too high for us to do nothing as their teachers. Our racialized Black and Brown students are read as dangerous and threatening by white mainstream U.S. society as they grow older, taller, and physically larger. Nasir's love of coffee and his urge to follow its scent rendered him dangerous in the eyes of the coffee cart owner and the police. He was read as a culpable adult, rather than an innocent child. His mother was able to use the English she knew to get him out of this particular situation—which was more dangerous for him than anyone else—but his safety should not depend on her English language skills or presence.

Teaching in a way that keeps our students as safe as possible is an obligation and responsibility that we have as teachers to all of our students. This safety concern is amplified for our racialized nonspeaking bilingual students. As educators, we want to let kids be kids, to be able to honor their interests and desires—like Nasir's for coffee. This also shows up in the ways we tend to hug young children in school and encourage them to hug adults in greeting when they are small and perceived as cute. Our students deserve affection and love, but we cannot confuse affection with infantilization. Students like Nasir become endangered as they grow older when we do not teach them about boundaries and consent toward other people's belongings. Students who love to hug become endangered as they grow older when we do not teach them about boundaries and consent toward other people's bodies and personal space. These young people may not always have an advocate with them, like Nasir did, to communicate and explain, and even if they do, that advocate may not be comfortable expressing themselves in English like Nasir's mother did. Rather than viewing this responsibility as belonging to the child or the parent, the responsibility should fall on society to rewire how we approach all people, and especially multilingual people with disabilities. Rather than immediately criminalizing Nasir, what might that interaction have looked like if the coffee cart owner and law enforcement officer were trained to understand and respect how different disabilities like autism manifest? What might that interaction have looked like if these two understood and respected that not all communication can and should happen in spoken English? The end goal is a society that honors all neurodiversity and forms of language expression, rather than demonizing it, but we are not there yet. In the interim, our classrooms need to be spaces that affirm children's interests, wants, and needs, while also teaching them strategies to engage with strangers and the public in a way that keeps them as safe as possible.

KEY IDEA(S)

What is language? What is communication? While these seem like simple questions, the varying perspectives on the answer lead to major breakdowns in communication and communicative justice in classrooms and places of learning. In broad terms, language and communication can be approached as transmissions of information, as a sharing of ideas, and as a process of comprehending one another. Box 2.1 offers questions to investigate how language and communication show up in your own classroom and learning spaces.

In this chapter, I explore various theories from a range of fields that address the question of how communication is defined, by whom, and to what end. I also explore texts that engage with the question of how early childhood communication is developed, how it is approached in formal learning spaces, and how disability, multilingualism, and racialization interact with perceptions of communication development. I examine several normative developmental models for communication development, including literature on systems of communication and gestural development to bring these pervasive perspectives into conversation with critical theories around languaging. I begin by presenting models to define communication,

Box 2.1. Invitation/Provocation/Offering: Defining Language and Communication in the Classroom

Invitation/Provocation/Offering—Respond to the following questions:

- How is language used in your classroom context? Give examples of what this looks and sounds like.
- How does communication occur in your classroom context? Give examples of what this looks and sounds like.

At the end of this chapter, we will return to this question to identify if and how your responses have shifted.

including different modalities of language (e.g., speech, gesture, sign) and critical perspectives that address social dynamics of languaging. Ultimately, the examination of these different theories provides an opportunity to explore and honor unspoken communication in its own right, yet the theories all fall short of explicitly addressing and centering multilingual nonspeaking subjects. I propose the use of elements of each theory to move toward communicative justice based on the experiences and expressions of nonspeaking multilingual children.

We have to know what various educational and medical professionals are claiming about communication in order to determine what to use and what to reject in our own teaching. One year when I taught a kindergarten, 1st-, and 2nd-grade self-contained special education class, I had a 2nd-grade student who rarely made eye contact. This particular student was not nonspeaking—in fact, he rarely stopped talking—but he was bilingual in Vietnamese and English. His IEP diagnosis was autism, and several of his IEP goals, which had been created by a district psychologist, centered around making eye contact during conversation. Several months into the school year, I met his parents at parent-teacher conferences. When I mentioned this goal, they looked confused. They shared with me that it was a cultural expectation in their home and community that he avoid eye contact while speaking with adults; this avoidance of eye contact was, for them, a sign of respect for one's elders. After that meeting, spurred by the cultural disconnect between the medical-educational professional goals and the family's teachings, I began doing my own research into eye contact during communication. I learned that for many students, particularly autistic students, having multiple forms of sensory input can actually detract from their ability to absorb information. For example, being forced to maintain eye contact during a conversation may negatively impact an individual's ability to take in and comprehend the auditory information directed at them. When I was speaking to this student of mine, he was better able to absorb my spoken words when he was *not* looking at me. This joined with his family's cultural expectations to make eye contact a completely inappropriate and ultimately harmful goal for his academic progress and communication development. Bilingualism is not just about spoken language; as we saw with this child and his family, it is also about nonverbal communication that intertwines with culture. Understanding nonverbal, unspoken communication dynamics can help us make our classrooms more inclusive, affirming spaces for all our children—speaking and nonspeaking, bilingual and monolingual alike.

Danesi (2022) summarized communication as the exchange and transmission of different messages. This transmission and exchange involve humans and can take place at the interpersonal level and the larger societal level. García et al. (2021) write about the possibilities for communication and languaging beyond dominant existing structures when they advocate for the following:

> The rights of racialized people to be educated on their own terms and on the basis of their own language practices. . . . a different world is already here—a world made by racialized bilinguals themselves as they engage with their own knowledge systems and cultural and linguistic practices (Martínez & Mejía, 2019). (García et al., 2021, p. 4)

This perspective, which challenges deficit thinking in languaging, is crucial to moving toward a more comprehensive framework for communication. In this chapter, I discuss the idea of *communicative justice*. Communicative justice is not a new idea, nor does it belong to me, though much of the current discourse centers on activism and media regarding adults (e.g., Pedro-Carañana et al., 2022) and does not center young children. I present communicative justice as an umbrella under which translanguaging; multimodal semiotics; alternative and augmentative communication supports; gesture; linguistic justice; developmental communicative components; and the intersection of translanguaging and universal design for learning (TrUDL), crip linguistics, and other theories of languaging fall. Communication at its core is about expression that is perceived and comprehended by another party in relative alignment with the intention of the person who is expressing. I explore language and communication ideologies that traffic through our schooling and learning spaces, both formal and informal and professional and familial, to unearth communication practices that are occurring in family relationships and to illustrate how schools and professional learning spaces might incorporate these knowledge systems, linguistic practices, and decolonial ways of "thinking otherwise" —and communicating otherwise. This thinking, being, and communicating "otherwise" is at the core of communicative justice. The umbrella visual (see Figure 2.1) represents my framing of the concept, further explored in this chapter.

While each of these theories is complex, nuanced, and important to explore in depth, I have summarized the crux of a few key concepts below. The theories that fall under the communicative justice umbrella here are not the only ones that make up communicative justice, but some core ones that support the expansion of communication for the benefit of nonspeaking bilingual children and all learners in the classroom.

Linguistic Justice

In her book *Linguistic Justice*, April Baker-Bell uplifts Black language, challenges excuses that the current language expectations in schools are "just the way it is" (2020, p. 7), and places Black language at the center of Black

Figure 2.1. Communicative Justice Umbrella

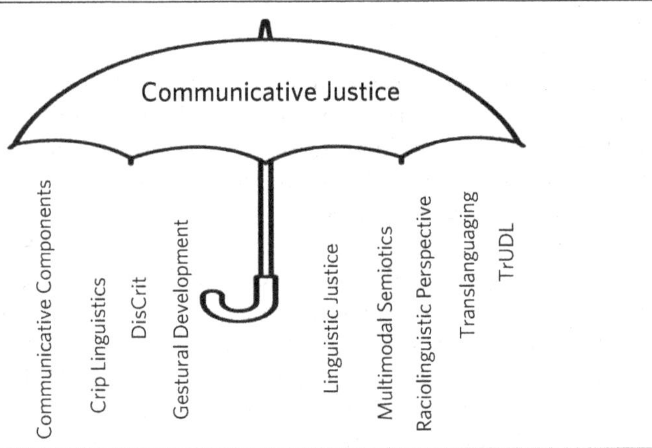

students' experiences and language education, countering the primacy of white mainstream English (WME) as the be-all and end-all for Black students. Communicative justice learns from Baker-Bell and this stance; in this book and this work, I challenge the idea that privileging spoken language is just the way it is and place multimodal, multilingual forms of language at the center of nonspeaking bilingual students' language education and experiences—and of all students' learning experiences. Decentering what I call white mainstream *spoken* English (WMSE) in our schools and lives is critical to more just, comprehensive teaching, learning, and being in the world.

Communicative Components

While typical developmental frameworks often reify a standardized monolingual English-speaking neurotypical middle- to upper-class individual, understanding the experiences of nonspeaking multilingual children in the context of these frameworks is important. Typical models of communication (Danesi, 2022; Jakobson, 1961; Shannon, 1949) give us the framing of an addresser (the person doing the expressing), the message (the information the addresser is sharing), the addressee (the person receiving the message), context (the situation), contact (the medium for the information to be shared), and code (the type of signal or sign being used; i.e., spoken language, written, GIFs, etc.). Though this model was developed for and has primarily been applied to verbal communication, it is applicable to nonverbal communication as well.

If we think back to the opening anecdote with Nasir, we can apply this traditional communication framework to the experience of a bilingual nonspeaking child.

Addresser: Nasir.
Message: Nasir wants the coffee in the cart.
Addressee: The coffee cart owner and the police officer.
Context: Nasir is both nonspeaking and bilingual. He is a Black child who is tall for his age. The coffee truck owner and the police officer have no knowledge of Nasir, his disability, or his communication.
Contact: Nonverbal physical interaction.
Code: Nasir physically went into the coffee truck owner's space seeking the coffee he desired.

As we saw with Nasir's case, the addressees (the coffee truck owner and the police officer) did not understand the contact and code Nasir used. They were all experiencing the same context, but because they did not have the same understanding of the context, they reacted to Nasir as if he were a threat, rather than reacting with understanding of the nonverbal code he was sending. Teachers often default to teaching WMSE because it seems to be the easiest way to help students be understood in society. In doing so, we inadvertently perpetuate the idea that nonverbal communication does not deserve to be understood in the same way WMSE does. I do not tell Nasir's story to encourage us to teach students like Nasir how to use WMSE; his story is a guiding light to help us begin to make change by questioning our own role as addressees. How do we understand our students? What contact and codes are we perceiving, and what contact and codes are we neglecting?

Crip Linguistics

Henner and Robinson (2021) wrote about "cripping" linguistics by centering disabled experiences and voices to rewire the way that we conceptualize language within and beyond the field of linguistics. The word *crip*, short for cripple(d), was originally used as a slur to demean disabled people, particularly those with physical disabilities. In the same way that many words that were originally derogatory have been reclaimed as a source of pride by communities who identify with the term, crip has been reclaimed by some disability justice activists and communities. Crip linguistics is one such example. Henner and Robinson (2021) advocated for us to remember that language is inextricably linked with the people using language. Part of their central argument is that speech is overly privileged in linguistics, and thus the use of non-speech languaging is labeled as deficit or inferior, and we must reorient this perspective. They draw heavily on research and experiences of D/deaf communities and signed languages. Deaf studies offers invaluable frameworks for deplatforming spoken language. According to Henner and

Robinson, "Crip linguistics, as a theory, encourages linguistics to reintegrate languaging with all bodies" (2021, p. 6).

I use crip linguistics in conversation with a raciolinguistic perspective (explored in Chapter 1) to reflect on educators' roles as perceiving subjects and communication partners with young nonspeaking bilingual children. Henner and Robinson (2021) also highlight that speech and spoken language are often used to draw distinctions between humans and animals. If spoken language is seen as the marker of humanity, what does that say about how we regard nonspeaking people? Even if we claim not to subscribe to those ideas, we can see how spoken language is privileged in schools as a marker of intelligence; communicating one's ideas through speech is one of the goals, with many national state standards incorporating "speaking and listening" standards. Crip linguistics helps us unsettle and reimagine not only how we understand communication, but how we conceptualize intelligence.

When I worked as a public school teacher and instructional coach in special education programs in New York City, I encountered principals who would assign the teachers they thought were bad instructors to the "nonverbal 6:1:1" classes. A *6:1:1* setting is one of the most restrictive in special education and means that there is a ratio of six students, one teacher, and one paraprofessional. Many of our 6:1:1 classes were made up primarily of nonspeaking students, as my first kindergarten class was. The assumption that a nonverbal 6:1:1 class was a punishment for "bad" teachers reinforces the notion that nonspeaking children are less intelligent and require less skill and capability from their educators. Crip linguistics reminds us that, in fact, the opposite is true. Nonspeaking children—and especially bilingual nonspeaking children—require educators who are not only skilled, perceptive partners, but who are able to cultivate classroom spaces that uplift, recognize, value, and utilize all forms of communication in the process of helping children expand into their fullest, most brilliant selves in the learning process.

Disability Critical Race Theory (DisCrit)

DisCrit—Disability Critical Race Theory—takes up an analysis of how disability and race intersect in the context of education. This theory, coined and popularized by Subini Annamma, Beth Ferri, and David Connor (2013), highlights how systems of power do not influence race and disability separately, so we must look at how disablement and racialization interact and intersect, and how people's lives are impacted by these intersections. DisCrit is fundamental to this book and to the theory of communicative justice because it helps us remember that issues of language are always connected to the people using the language, and disability and race are inextricably linked to how people live their lives—and how they use their language.

DisCrit provides a foundation for thinking about disability, race, and language within the systems of power that govern our schools and our lives. Nasir's experience with the coffee cart highlights how inextricably linked race, language, and disability are. The fact that Nasir, a Black nonspeaking bilingual child, was read as a threat and pushed to the ground by a cop cannot be separated from the racial profiling that Black men experience at the hands of law enforcement officers in the United States.

Raciolinguistic Perspective

A raciolinguistic perspective, which was introduced briefly in Chapter 1, is concerned with how racial identities factor into communication, and specifically how students' communication is policed, perceived, and valued in educational settings. The student, in Flores and Rosa's 2015 conceptualization of a raciolinguistic perspective, is a racialized subject, whose language and expression is read through the lens of a white listening subject, whose understandings of what qualifies as appropriate, proper, formal, academic, and valuable speech determine how a student is understood and received. This framework is crucial to this work because it reminds us to keep race at the heart of the work, as race influences how different acts of communication are perceived and responded to—especially in school settings. As you will see in Chapters 3 and 4, the way that the Latine families in the study perceive their children's communication is very different from the way the educators—the white listening subjects—perceive the children's communication. The white listening subject does not have to be white but represents the ideals of whiteness in relation to speaking and expression.

One example that I think of with the white listening subject that applies raciolinguistics beyond speaking and listening is when people kiss in greeting as a salutation. I worked in a school that was entirely special education classes, where all the children had IEPs. One of the schoolwide rules for appropriate behavior was "We don't kiss in school." Kissing was read as something inappropriate and invasive, something that did not belong in a learning space (Padía & Traxler, 2020). When I first started teaching, I enforced this rule, thinking that I was supporting my students in learning appropriate, respectful behavior. One day, I noticed my paraprofessionals kissing each other on the cheek in greeting when we got to school in the morning. Something clicked for me. When I enforced the "We don't kiss in school" rule, I played the role of the white listening subject. I was reading students' actions as inappropriate, when the reality was that kissing on the cheek in greeting was something expected in their homes, communities, and cultures. While a cheek kiss is not a spoken phrase or word that someone can "hear" literally, it is an action and a form of expression. The way that

I—and the school policy—responded to that expression was a form of *listening*, and because we were policing that expression and labeling it as wrong or deviant in the school space, we were imposing white cultural values. We were playing the role of the white listening subjects—even those of us who were not white. This raciolinguistic perspective will help us throughout this book and in our work as educators to understand how our perception and *listening* of our students is racialized, and how we can unlearn and relearn to be more attentive, humble communication partners, to honor the communication of our students.

Translanguaging

Translanguaging as a theory has become more well known in the last several years in teacher education, teacher development, and curriculum design, particularly in areas with lots of multilingual students and bilingual/dual-language programs. Translanguaging, at its core, is the idea that we all have one linguistic repertoire that we use to make meaning. Historically, linguists have described bilingual people as having two separate cognitive systems for their first language (L1) and second language (L2). Translanguaging challenges this concept and holds that all bilingual people have one system where they store all their meaning-making tools. Translanguaging is often confused with *code-switching*, wherein a person moves between two languages or dialects depending on the audience they are engaging with. Translanguaging might include code-switching, because this act of choosing which language tools to use in a given moment is part of the process of using all the tools we house in our singular linguistic repertoire.

A person who uses Spanglish might be translanguaging, as might a person who uses a mix of Spanish and English in one sentence to get their meaning across, as might a person who is bilingual but is solely communicating in Spanish at a moment in time. Just because a child is not speaking does not mean they are not making meaning. And as they make meaning of the world, both in terms of what they comprehend and in terms of how they present themselves and their ideas, they are using their one, full linguistic repertoire to communicate. They are translanguaging, in multiple modalities and within multiple named languages.

THE STATUS QUO: PROBLEMATIC CURRENT PRACTICES

There is a parallel history in the United States of special education and bilingual education (Alsace & Colón, 2022). Several laws in this country have attempted to protect and implement inclusive and special education, such as the 1975 Education for All Handicapped Children Act, the multiple iterations of the Individuals with Disabilities Education Act (IDEA), and the Every Student Succeeds Act (ESSA). Other advocates and lawmakers have focused on the implementation of bilingual education. One of the prominent court cases commonly referenced in bilingual education history in the United States is *Lau v. Nichols*, in which a 1974 Supreme Court ruling established that language programs for students who were not considered proficient in English were necessary to provide equal educational opportunities to all (Baker & Wright, 2017). The Every Student Succeeds Act (ESSA) and its reauthorization in 2015 addressed English language proficiency, though it was listed as a distinct demographic and need from special or inclusive education. Alsace and Colón identify that

> Not surprisingly, finding data on academic results for ELL/SWD [English Language Learners/Students with Disabilities] since the inception of ESSA is also next to impossible, especially given the challenges posed by the COVID-19 pandemic for obtaining accurate academic achievement information in general. (2022, p. xxxiii)

Students at the intersections of bilingual education and special education often have their needs met in the bucket of special education *or* bilingual education, but rarely at this important nexus (Cioè-Peña, 2017; Ehlers-Zavala, 2011). Bilingual special education programming is limited, in part because there is a shortage of teachers and related service providers who are certified to provide both special education and bilingual education services (Wang & Woolf, 2015). As such, children who are labeled as both disabled and as English learners or multilingual learners rarely experience formal education that attends to their full selves.

Along with the history of laws for bilingual and special education and the certification trends that influence children's schooling experiences, the history of language and labels plays a major role in our cultural approaches to disability and multilinguals in schools today. Among my friend group, I am known for getting upset when the word *dumb* is used in a derogatory way. This is because I have found that once you learn the ableist origins of a word or idea, it is impossible to leverage it in the same way. When I learned the history of the word dumb, I was shocked and upset. *Merriam-Webster* lists the following definitions for the word dumb:

> 1a: lacking intelligence: STUPID
> b: showing a lack of intelligence
> c: requiring no intelligence
> 2a: lacking the human power of speech
> b: dated, offensive, of a person . . . : lacking the ability to speak: MUTE

3: temporarily unable to speak (as from shock or astonishment)
4: not expressed in uttered words
5: SILENT
6: lacking some usual attribute or accompaniment
7: not having the capability to process data (Merriam-Webster, 2024)

As you can see, there are a mix of definitions, ranging from lacking intelligence to absence of speech. This is no coincidence. The term originally meant lacking spoken language, both permanent and temporary, and it evolved into referring to people who were considered to be not so smart as "dumb." The implications here are huge. When we conflate intelligence with spoken language, we miss all of the beautiful ways that humans—and our students—express creativity, genius, joy, and brilliance.

I spent some time on a farm in Mexico writing this book. When I told the owner of the farm what the book was about, he said, "Nonverbal bilingual children. That almost sounds like an oxymoron." And that's the thing—most educators would likely say the same. This is precisely why this work is so important. Nonspeaking bilingual children may not be considered bilingual when it comes to their use of *spoken* language, but they are *bilingual people.* They communicate across two languages in their daily lives, but because we cannot measure their comprehension or expression using our typical systems that rely on spoken language, we struggle to comprehend both their general knowledge but also their bilingualism. Our work as educators is to figure out how to fix our classrooms, our pedagogy, and our perceptive skills to create more space for these children to be and express all of who they are. They are always existing as themselves, as bilingual beings, but it is not always the case that we recognize and honor their full selves in the classroom.

LEARNINGS FROM CHILDREN, FAMILIES, AND EDUCATORS

One student I worked with used a tablet to type his responses to questions. During a math activity, I asked him to solve an addition equation: 20 + 6. Instead of pressing the numeral buttons to indicate 26, he typed out "veinti-six." In Spanish, the word for 26 is *veintiseis*. In English it is 26. He was translanguaging, using his full linguistic repertoire and his nonspoken mode of communicating via his tech device. He embodied what Cioè-Peña (2021b) calls Translanguaging Universal Design for Learning (TrUDL). TrUDL identifies the need to not only include just multilingual, translanguaging opportunities in the classroom, but also integrate those with Universal Design for Learning (UDL; CAST, 2024). This approach seeks to remedy the disconnect between special education services and multilingual supports in schools, which are often viewed as discrete practices or strategies or types of servicing belonging to different practitioners in the school setting. TrUDL advocates for us to conceptualize approaches to teaching and learning as both multimodal (a UDL approach) and multilingual (a translanguaging approach). We must consider how we as educators can create more opportunities for students to use their meaning-making tools and their expressive tools across named languages and modalities, lest we miss the brilliance of a student who is able to share that he got the answer "veinti-six."

Multiple educators and early intervention providers in this study used the expression of *language exploding* for the young bilingual nonspeaking/minimally speaking children they worked with. The language of *explosion* was used to convey excitement for what occurred with oral language development. When children who were previously considered language-delayed or nonverbal started to speak in words, phrases, and sentences, educators expressed joy and enthusiasm for how their communication had evolved. What if we were able to understand rapid language development and expression outside of spoken words? Could it be that children's other forms of languaging are also *exploding* or growing at a rapid pace, but we are not equipped to perceive them, and/or we do not value these growth spurts in the same way? Kayla, an early intervention provider, mentioned how much Hector grew during her time working with him in sessions, citing his growth in terms of his oral language. She said, "Like wow, he just really really . . . grew . . . speaking a lot more in full sentences, answering questions, being able to engage in a back-and-forth."

Hector began early intervention services because his mother identified that he was not communicating with spoken words the way that children his age were expected to. This was true in both Spanish and English; while he responded to communication in English from his parents and Spanish from his grandparents, he responded with gestures, facial expressions, and vocalizations like laughter or cries. His mother was concerned that he was not attempting to use spoken words, nor was he babbling the way his cousins did as they began to talk. As Hector spent more time with his early intervention providers, he began to use spoken English. That Kayla's main focus was spoken language when asked about his growth is no surprise. Our systems of education prioritize spoken English language as a criterion of success in the United States.

While it makes sense to express enthusiasm about students' growth in language skills that are widely understood, it is also important that we challenge WMSE as the ultimate goal for communication. Why does a child have to use oral language to engage in a back-and-forth? What does it mean to engage in a back-and-forth without oral words? How can we notice, observe, perceive, value, and measure communication beyond spoken words—and specifically beyond WMSE?

COMMUNICATIVE JUSTICE TAKEAWAYS

Communication can have many different definitions. Generally, authentic communication is interpreted as intentional communication by one party that is perceived by another party in relative alignment with the expressed intent. *Who gets to define communication? Is it the perceiving subject? How do we decide when perception matches intent, particularly if the expressing subject does not speak to confirm or deny that the perception aligns with their intended meaning?*

Literature that engages translanguaging identifies meaning-making, as does literature on social and multimodal semiotics. *Who gets to make meaning in our classrooms? How do we ensure that meaning is co-constructed, rather than just imposed by us as educators—the perceiving subjects?* In special education, independence is often touted as the ultimate goal for students, both in terms of their individualized education program annual goals and in terms of least restrictive environment and the content curriculum (Padía & Traxler, 2020). This notion of independence also permeates normative discourses on communication and positions communication as the responsibility of the individual who is sharing an idea, rather than a collective experience between two or more parties. Children like Nasir and Hector are held accountable for the way that they use—or *fail* to use—WMSE. The communication partners who misinterpret or misunderstand them are rarely held accountable for their failure to understand the nonverbal communication being shared.

Examining the role of interdependence is essential in exploring communication. Research on early childhood development indicates that social interaction with adults and peers not only has positive impacts on cognitive skills development, but also positively impacts young children's confidence levels and modes of communication (Kington et al., 2013). Expanding our conceptions of communication beyond spoken named languages is essential in the cognitive and social communicative development of children. One of the principles of disability justice, as stated by the disability rights collective Sins Invalid, reads, "We meet each others' needs as we build toward liberation, knowing that state solutions inevitably extend into further control over lives" (2018). School solutions are state solutions for the most part. In addition, we must question what it means to meet each other's needs when the needs of those who are nonspeaking are so often unrecognized by speaking people.

The Communication Bill of Rights, produced by the American Speech–Language–Hearing Association (ASHA), outlines some elements of communication that all individuals should be entitled to as communicative rights. It states,

> All people with a disability of any extent or severity have a basic right to affect, through communication, the conditions of their existence. Beyond this general right, a number of specific communication rights should be ensured in all daily interactions and interventions involving persons who have severe disabilities. To participate fully in communication interactions, each person has these fundamental communication rights:
>
> 1. The right to interact socially, maintain social closeness, and build relationships
> 2. The right to request desired objects, actions, events, and people
> 3. The right to refuse or reject undesired objects, actions, events, or choices
> 4. The right to express personal preferences and feelings
> 5. The right to make choices from meaningful alternatives
> 6. The right to make comments and share opinions
> 7. The right to ask for and give information, including information about changes in routine and environment
> 8. The right to be informed about people and events in one's life
> 9. The right to access interventions and supports that improve communication
> 10. The right to have communication acts acknowledged and responded to even when the desired outcome cannot be realized
> 11. The right to have access to functioning AAC (augmentative and alternative communication) and other AT (assistive technology) services and devices at all times
> 12. The right to access environmental contexts, interactions, and opportunities that promote participation as full communication partners with other people, including peers
> 13. The right to be treated with dignity and addressed with respect and courtesy
> 14. The right to be addressed directly and not be spoken for or talked about in the third person while present
> 15. The right to have clear, meaningful, and culturally and linguistically appropriate communications. (Brady et al., 2016, p. 123)

"The right to access interventions and supports that improve communication" (#9) can be interpreted in many ways. If a nonspeaking individual is part of an organization or institution that believes that improved communication is synonymous with typically perceived spoken English, then the "rights" that a person is afforded and the interventions that fall under this purview may very well be violent and disrespectful of the person's wholeness. If Nasir's teachers believed that what happened to him at the coffee cart was because he could not communicate using WMSE, the following classroom interventions would be geared toward developing his spoken English language. For a child like Nasir, he may never develop spoken English language, so these goals are dismissive of who he is as a person and how he *does* communicate. When we only measure children by what they cannot do, we fail to honor their true, whole selves.

This circles back to the questions (1) *What is communication?* and (2) *Who gets to define communication and how it is expected/enacted/taught/perceived/valued?* It also raises questions like: *How do nonspeaking people get their needs and wants met, and how do they enact agency in a world largely premised on spoken communication*?

AAC devices offer a multimodal approach to communication, but their use is still seen as primarily a tool and companion to support verbal/vocal communication. Gesture development and AAC device use are often parts of a trajectory moving an individual toward developing more vocal speech production/expression. Crais et al. (2004) posit that knowing which function typically emerges first may help clinicians target the most viable communication function to associate with early intervention activities. They point out that only half of gestures between 8 and 11 months are accompanied by vocalizations, and that typically gestures are overtaken by vocal speech as a child grows older. Gesture, according to Crais and colleagues (2004), is used as a tool to evaluate where on the hierarchy of gestural development a child is in order to assess the deficits and subsequent delays in language production. Their proposed hierarchy of behaviors for requesting objects is as follows:

1. looking;
2. vocalizing;
3. vocalizing and looking;
4. making contact with an adult's hand;
5. reaching with whole hand;
6. reaching with whole hand and vocalizing;
7. reaching with opening and closing hand;
8. reaching with opening and closing hand while vocalizing;
9. pointing, looking at the object, at the adult, and then at the object; and
10. using a word/word approximation.

Here it is clear that the ultimate and desired behavior for requesting an object is using a spoken word or word approximation. Any child that falls behind these metrics is identified as "at risk" and/or deficient, and often referred for specialized services and interventions. Early childhood teachers are often required to administer developmental screeners and/or kindergarten readiness assessments that include evaluations of a child's speech according to "typical" speech and language milestones.

Some social signs—sometimes referred to as social semiotics—have different significance and salience across named languages and cultures, which might impact the experience of communication partnership for nonspeaking multilingual children. For example, in some cultures people point with their mouths and/or faces to draw a communication partner's attention to a person, place, object, or occurrence. If a communication partner is unfamiliar with this physical sign, meaning-making and perception of expression is compromised. Similarly, I have experienced standardized exams where children are provided with pictures of lifeguards, and the red and white cross on the swimsuit is supposed to support the children's comprehension in accessing the text about swimming. For children who are not familiar with this symbol, and/or who come from cultures or nation-states where this symbol is not used for lifeguards, they may assume the sign is referring to clergy or something church-related. Semiotics and critical analyses of multimodal social semiotics offer elements of nonspoken communication that are important to consider for communicative justice, but the literature often falls short in addressing these cultural considerations.

We cannot make the mistake of assuming that the use of visuals automatically makes a lesson or activity more accessible for nonspeaking children. In the same way that sites like Google Translate may have errors related to different versions of Spanish or different cultural contexts, visuals vary largely in how legible they are to any given person; the context of both the culture and the sentence matter. I was translating a document related to special education once and did not know the word for *accommodations* (in terms of IEP accommodations) in Spanish. Google Translate told me the word was *alojamientos* and offered no other alternatives. *Alojamientos* are physical accommodations, where one might sleep. I have similarly seen visuals of trees that children misinterpret to be broccoli because of how they are drawn. The use of visuals is integral to expansive communication, but so is our analysis of the relationship between culture, context, and the visuals we are engaging.

To work toward communicative justice in our learning spaces, we must consider not only how expressive communication is happening but how receptive understanding is experienced by the *listening*—or perceiving or interpreting—subject. We must move toward a more expansive framework of meaning-making that centers nonspoken linguistic tools and nonspeaking bilingual children.

"Language minoritized" children, as they are discussed and identified in the current translanguaging literature (e.g., Blommaert et al., 2018), are written about with the assumption that they use spoken language(s). Nonspeaking multilingual children are doubly language minoritized, both in terms of named language(s) and in terms of modality of expression.

Despite this thread of hegemonic spoken language, there are spaces where translanguaging theory opens doors for analyzing and transforming linguistic oppression for nonspeaking multilingual children. For example, it can be applied to highlight the way that nonspeaking emergent bilingual students are literally forced, through systems like AAC devices being programmed solely in English, to select and use features corresponding to dominant practices.

> . . . our understandings of translanguaging goes beyond the linguistic system itself to incorporate doing language, which means assembling, as Pennycook (2017) has said, the linguistic and multimodal practices that speakers have acquired through social interaction, as well as their embodied cognition. Since the speaker's lexical and structural resources constitute only a small part of this assemblage, translanguaging not only posits a single linguistic system, a single set of linguistic resources, but also goes well beyond it to encompass a communicative repertoire that is often seen as outside of what traditionally is defined as "linguistic." (García & Otheguy, 2020, p. 26)

In most research on multimodal signs that bilingual students use, these signs are analyzed through a translanguaging lens in conjunction with their spoken linguistic features. Often, multimodal or nonverbal signs are seen by theorists and educators as partners with linguistic spoken features. This conception of translanguaging also addresses how students make meaning in relation to and with their bodies. This approach is important because it highlights the ways that bilingual students make meaning with their bodies and outside of their bodies beyond linguistic signs and linguistic markers. García and Otheguy also claim that "At the same time, it is important to help bilingual students understand that named languages are co-present in their lives in schools" (2020, p. 27). Is there any escaping this for bilingual nonverbal students? Many communication pedagogies are premised on supporting students in accessing the dominant named languages. Exploring how families communicate may help illuminate how schools can move away from this trap. There is a growing—yet still small—body of research that hones in on the experiences of families of students labeled as disabled who are also multilingual in the context of U.S. schooling.

One of my students who is an early childhood educator made a comment that she felt so sad when she read the Communication Bill of Rights—sad that we need a guiding document reminding us of these rights. What if we enacted communicative justice in schools in ways that honor all of us? As I told my students, even those of us with the best intentions don't always have positive impacts. For educators concerned with justice, it is important that we look at whether our impact aligns with our intentions. When we look at the Communication Bill of Rights, one of the rights is to be spoken to directly, rather than spoken about. I have definitely fallen into the trap of speaking to my colleagues about a student in their presence, despite my fierce commitment to communicative justice. We will make mistakes. What is most important is that we reflect on our actions, recognize when certain moments are mistakes, and learn from them to transform our learning spaces into sites of liberatory languaging.

Lisa Delpit's foundational work on the *culture of power* (1995) says,

> 1. Issues of power are enacted in classrooms.
> 2. There are codes or rules for participating in power; that is, there is a "culture of power."
> 3. The rules of the culture of power are a reflection of the rules of the culture of those who have power.
> 4. If you are not already a participant in the culture of power, being told explicitly the rules of that culture makes acquiring power easier.
> 5. Those with power are frequently least aware of—or least willing to acknowledge—its existence. Those with less power are often most aware of its existence. (p. 282)

We live in a certain culture of power. Teaching the rules of the culture of power does not mean teaching that said culture of power is correct, superior, ideal, or even desirable. It can err on that side if we are not explicit about this culture of power. But when we teach our students that the culture of power exists, when we name the rules of the culture of power and we express that this is not the ideal or primary way to be, but rather one of many ways of being and acting—and one that might be expected in certain spaces—we are helping our students develop the tools to participate in the culture of power should they so choose, while also helping them think metacognitively about the ways that power functions, the ways culture functions, and how they choose to enact, embody, and communicate themselves. The culture of power has been taken up by many educators to advocate for more expansive uses of spoken language in schools. I urge us to consider how the culture of power when it comes to language can also be used to think more expansively, beyond spoken words, to consider a wide range of communication practices. There were videos that went viral in recent years of teachers who had visual choice boards outside their classroom doors for morning greetings. Students would line up and as they approached the classroom door, would gesture to or touch the image that represented the type of greeting they preferred that day. Options included a high five, a handshake, a hug, a wave, and a dance. Having visual communication boards with options like these that include both pictures or photographs and written words in multiple languages is one representation of honoring student agency, expansive

Box 2.2. Provocation, Revisited

After reading this chapter, respond to the following questions again (if possible, use a new piece of paper or a new document; do not look at your previous answers just yet):

- How can language be used in more expansive ways in your classroom context? Give examples of how you might incorporate this.
- How can you remind yourself to notice the various ways communication occurs in your classroom context? How can you ensure that you encourage and create space for all these forms of communication?

communication, while still orienting students to the culture of power that expects them to engage in some sort of initial greeting or salutation in the morning. (Of course, if students do not feel like greeting their teacher at all, that should be their prerogative, but this is one example of how choice can be constructed within the culture of power that dominates our schools and our society at large.)

When it comes to language use and linguistic norms, I always advocate for teaching that there are multiple ways to communicate, and just because a certain way might be privileged in an academic setting does not mean that it is the superior way to communicate; it just means that it is the mode that is valued the most in certain systems. Providing spaces for our students to use their full linguistic repertoires, while also being transparent with them about which ways of languaging are valued in certain spaces, can help students make their own determinations about their languaging.

In the section that follows, there are some protocols and guiding questions to help you ensure you are recognizing and creating space for various forms of language and expression in your classroom or learning community.

TEACHING IN ACTION

The Culture of Power and Communicative Justice in the Classroom

The concept of the culture of power is framed in these reflection activities in terms of power and communication in your own classroom. In the Communicative Justice in Action: Expansive Linguistic Repertoires Protocol below, you will find a roadmap for considering and including expansive linguistic repertoires in your classroom community. In Box 2.3, you will explore power and communicative justice in your classroom with your students. Be sure to use what you noticed during the CJA: Expansive Linguistic Repertoires Protocol to plan for your group discussion. You want to include all students' voices, in whatever form they take, into your classroom discourse. Include prompts in all the languages that your students use, and if you have students who use communication devices or assistive technology, be sure to prepare vocabulary boards, program their devices with the necessary words and phrases, and plan to incorporate visuals as much as possible into your group discussion.

Communicative Justice in Action: Expansive Linguistic Repertoires Protocol

1. Observe and document how students respond to any given prompt.
2. No matter how they express their answer (spoken words, written words, drawings, gestures, use of visuals), affirm that they did an amazing job communicating their thoughts.
3. Then ask the class if they can think of additional ways to express or share the same information.
4. Integrate this practice into your daily learning routine. Whether it is supporting a classroom community in developing their multilingualism, their multidialecticalism (use of one or more dialects of the same formal language), and/or their multimodal expression, working as a learning community to express the same idea in multiple ways can ensure that we are modeling for students multiple ways for them to express themselves and multiple ways for them to understand and perceive others who may communicate in different ways than they do themselves.

Establishing these understandings with students can go a long way toward generating trust and classroom community. If I had used protocols like these with my student Veronica (from Chapter 1's opening anecdote), I could have shared with her that there are times when the expectation is to write her journal entry with no erasing, and there are other times when it is okay to take her time and erase and rewrite as much as she would like. Sharing these communication expectations helps students understand that they are not being chastised for who they are and how they express themselves but are being given clear directions about how to communicate on specific tasks at specific times. Sharing with students that there are many different, valuable ways to communicate is crucial; we must be transparent

Box. 2.3. Culture of Power and Communicative Justice Exercise

Use the following prompts below to engage this conversation with your students. You may adjust the questions depending on the age group you are working with. Modalities may include group discussion/brainstorm, small-group discussions/graphic organizers, individual free-writes, recording a podcast episode discussing the issue, and so on.

Prompt:

1) What is the "Culture of Power" when it comes to language?
   a) Differentiated: What are the different ways that people communicate at school? (Spoken, written, AAC devices, gestures, facial expressions, etc.)
   b) How do YOU like to communicate? (Can point, choose from field of 2, use device to indicate, etc.).
2) What are the rules of language in (your) school or site?
   a) Differentiated: How are you "supposed" to communicate in your classroom? (Can point, choose from a field of two options, use a device, etc.)

Follow-ups:

1) How are you expected to "talk" at school or at your site?
2) How do you know? What happens when you do not talk like this?
3) How are you expected to write at school or at your site?
4) How do you know? What happens when you do not write like this?
5) How are you expected to share your feelings and thoughts at school or at your site?
6) How do you know? What happens when you do not share your feelings in this way?
7) Create anchor charts together with the School/Site Language Culture of Power. You may want to brainstorm times when students may choose and/or be expected to use these linguistic standards (e.g., for state tests [essay portion], during identified homework activities, etc.).

Then create anchor charts with Our Classroom Language Culture, and have students walk through all the different ways that they speak (Spanglish, Arabish, Chinglish, body language, texting/emojis, translanguaging, etc.). Identify times when they may choose and/or be expected to use this—certain classroom presentations, classroom discussions, Do Nows, journal entries, homework assignments, for instance.

Start to be explicit with your students when assignments are given. Is there a certain language practice they are expected to engage in for this assignment? If so, give them handouts that are mini copies of the anchor chart(s) and tell them they can use these as guideposts. If the assignment is one that will have multiple revisions, perhaps tell them to use whatever classroom language culture they prefer to communicate themselves, but also let them know that at some point they will be editing using the School/Site Language Culture of Power.

with students that there are certain languages of power that are expected and used in schools, and while we do teach those to our students at times, those are not the only, nor are they the "correct" ways to communicate. They are merely options in the wide, expansive range of communication tools we have at our disposal.

CHAPTER 3

Beyond the Bilingual Confusion Trope

> If the research highlights all of the gains to be made from being bilingual, why do EBLADs [emergent bilinguals labeled as disabled] continue to be placed in monolingual settings? Are program options being decided based on student need, family interest and the linguistic realities in which they live? Or are these decisions based on a normalizing bias that leads to an external evaluator deciding what is appropriate for an Other based on their measure of what is normal and what is not?
>
> —María Cioè-Peña

FORCED TO CHOOSE: BILINGUALISM OR MONOLINGUAL SPECIAL EDUCATION

Several coworkers and friends of mine, all of whom are teachers, have shared with me over the years that they lied on the Home Language Questionnaire (HLQ) that's given to families upon school intake. They lied to say that English was the only language spoken in their home. The reason for this is that the HLQ asks parents/guardians to identify whether any language other than English is spoken in the home, and if the answer is yes, the child is automatically tested for "English language proficiency." This is the case even if the parent or guardian notes that the child does not speak any language other than English; if anyone else in the home is noted to speak another language, it triggers an evaluation process for English learner status. My bilingual friends who have children who have already been identified with disabilities and/or delays when they enter the public school system are especially wary of checking this box, because they know their children might struggle with testing, not because of language, but because of their disability. When I asked about their choice, one friend told me that it was not because she didn't want bilingual services for her child, but that she knew bilingual special education services were rarely available. What would happen to her son, she said, was he would get labeled as an English learner, given little to no supports for bilingualism and biliteracy, and viewed as less capable by many people. She would rather he receive services and supports for his disability in the language she knew he was guaranteed to receive instruction in—English—even if this meant that his bilingual development got stunted. The reality that many parents are forced to prioritize monolingual English special education services over bilingual supports—and the fact that these monolingual English special education services are far more available than quality bilingual special education services—speaks to the failure of our school system to support and honor children who live at the intersections of bilingualism and disability.

One year when I worked as an instructional coach, I was tasked with administering the state English Language Proficiency exam that students labeled as English learners were required to take each year. Only when students scored "proficient" on the test did they stop taking this exam each year. The school I worked in was all students with IEPs. The test had four components: Speaking, Listening, Reading, and Writing. I was required to proctor this for all of our students, and the test was not modified at all. Administering this test to my nonspeaking bilingual students was such a painful experience. Because the Speaking portion required spoken English words from students, I was forced to share the questions with the students and mark "no response" over and over. The fact that our schools use standardized tests that claim to measure language ability but do not account for multiple forms of language expression shows just how marginalized our nonspeaking bilingual children are. There was no possibility of a bilingual nonspeaking student passing an exam like that, because in order to pass, they would need to use spoken language.

KEY IDEA(S)

School professionals, including administrators, teachers, psychologists, and other related service providers, often position bilingualism as too complex and confusing for neurodivergent students. Parents and guardians are often counseled toward monolingual special education under this premise that bilingualism will deter or further delay their children's academic development. However, bilingualism is *not* too confusing for disabled children, because they are bilingual people who live bilingual lives. When we prioritize monolingual English communication and schooling for nonspeaking bilingual children, we prioritize white monolingual English standards of communication and community and deprioritize the reality of bilingual nonspeaking children's lives.

The linguistic ideologies that govern and dictate formal schooling and service spaces for our bilingual nonspeaking children have deep implications for communicative justice. On the one hand, many families and educators want to give their children access to the culture of power (Delpit, 1995), which in the current moment means spoken English language. On the other hand, families use multiple named languages (in the case of the families in this book, English and Spanish) as well as communicative acts like gesture, physical touch, visual cues, and more that extend far beyond the reach of spoken English language. When our schools and related service spaces offer monolingual English programming and/or steer families away from bi/multilingual education, they are reifying the idea that there is one superior way to communicate: through spoken "standard" English language, or WMSE. This ideology negates space for educators and families to collaborate together to share communicative practices outside of these narrow boundaries. The first step toward linguistic justice is to identify that this WMSE linguistic ideology governs our schooling and learning spaces; the second step is to challenge this ideology with other options and approaches that affirm a multimodal translanguaging; the third step is for children, their families, and their educators to collaborate to share and build communicative practices that expand our perceptive capacities.

As educators, one of the most important things that we can do for children and families is to recognize their full communicative repertoires, and also recognize the robust communication systems that families develop that are often ignored, marginalized, or invalidated in professional learning spaces. This is particularly relevant when working with families of emergent bilingual nonspeaking children or children who receive speech and language services. These young people are often considered doubly deficient, and their families are rarely given options or seen as experts when it comes to their language use and development. Another way that educators can disrupt the deficit view of bilingual nonspeaking children and their families is by recognizing the range of cultural and linguistic capital that families have and bring. Many of the systems and communicative practices that families engage with and create involve multilingual and multimodal expression; taking a cue from families' practices could lead our schooling away from the siloed options of bilingual education *or* English as a New Language services *or* monolingual special education, and move us toward communicative justice in *all* our learning spaces.

THE STATUS QUO: PROBLEMATIC CURRENT PRACTICES

One of the greatest myths that exists is that bilingualism is too confusing for kids with disabilities and impedes progress for students who are delayed according to standardized cognitive metrics (Artiles & Ortiz, 2002). The notion that being bilingual detracts from one's ability to progress cognitively is rooted in white supremacy and ableism. In actuality, research shows that children who experience bilingual and biliterate education are more likely to demonstrate success and improvement in English than children who are bilingual but only receive educational supports/classes in English (Cummins, 1984; Ortiz, 1984). The intersection of this bilingual confusion trope with the lack of educational personnel who are themselves bilingual leads to systems that perpetuate monolingual English programs and services for students with disabilities. Do our fields claim that this is best because we are attempting to convince ourselves and families that our systems are adequate when we know we are strategically underresourced and underprepared, or do we genuinely believe that monolingual learning is superior to bilingual learning? It may be some combination of both, or that the two have become so intertwined because of how pervasive the medical model of disability is that attempts to "fix" any ways of thinking and being outside of normalized standards, as well as a raciolinguistic ideology that reveres English and identifies all other languages as inferior—particularly for non-white children.

LEARNINGS FROM CHILDREN, FAMILIES, AND EDUCATORS

Language, Power, and Stigma

Different families in the study had different experiences when it came to accessing bilingual service and education options. Table 3.1 outlines the different early intervention and/or special education services the children received and the language(s) of instruction.

Fiona talked about her son not liking Spanish and telling his parents not to speak it, despite it being the primary language that her parents—her son's grandparents—speak, including with him. She also lamented the fact that he doesn't know Spanish, sharing that she feels more comfortable in Spanish than in English, and she knows that it's part of his culture so she should probably teach it to him. She spent most of the interview talking about how hard she had to fight to get him services for early intervention (EI) and the process of getting him special education. While she did not explicitly state this, I wonder if the possibility of bilingual education/programming on top of this might feel even more overwhelming, since she has already had such an uphill battle with medical and educational professionals. She did, however, identify one EI provider who spoke with her son in both languages, citing that he had offered it because he was bilingual himself, from Puerto Rico, and felt more comfortable in Spanish.

Reading what Fiona shared through a lens of testimonio—a first-person account from someone who experienced an event or condition, usually related to oppression or marginalization—highlights the nature of the either/or

Table 3.1. Service(s) Received and Language(s) of Service

Child	Child's Age	Identity/Notes	Caregiver	Educator Name and Title/Profession	Services Received	Language(s) of Service(s)
Bernardo	3	One white American, one Mexican parent; primarily Spanish spoken at home.	Florence, university faculty/ science researcher	Kaitlin, preschool teacher	Preschool inclusive instruction	English; Kaitlin noted that some teachers know some Spanish and will try to use it.
Emmanual	9	Family is bilingual, and grandparents speak only Spanish; Emmanual does not speak but increasingly seems to understand.	Susana, bilingual elementary school teacher	Marilyn, special education teacher	Occupational therapy, speech therapy, special education—self-contained and inclusive ed	English
Hector	3	Colombian-American; mom's first language is Spanish, and grandparents speak only Spanish to him, but he says "No Spanish" when mom speaks it to him. He replies in English.	Fiona, completing degree in psychology; considering pathways to teaching	Kayla, ABA therapist, early Intervention	Speech therapy, ABA therapy	English ABA therapy, Spanish speech therapy (unofficially)
Katrina	4	Did not participate, but mom and SLP shared about her development	Katherine, bilingual elementary school teacher	Ofelia, bilingual SLP	Speech therapy	English and Spanish
Niveyah	4	Nonspeaking; family uses both English and Spanish and self-described "Spanglish." Exhibits echolalia but primarily just in English. Watches videos and plays tablet games in both languages.	Lianna, works in the home	Ofelia, bilingual SLP	Speech therapy	English and Spanish

divide in bi/multilingualism and disability–special education. She had to put so much energy into fighting for access to early intervention and special education supports that it seems Hector's bilingualism fell by the wayside. His bilingualism—and specifically his Spanish language—became roadkill as she navigated the pothole and barrier-filled terrain of the path to disability supports. The lack of bilingual options that were provided to her are a systemic problem, but it is so entrenched in our culture for blame to be situated with parents. Whether parents/caregivers have internalized that blame or that blame is projected onto them by professionals, this is a narrative that must be rewritten.

I also wonder if parents/caregivers are more hesitant to enroll their children in bilingual programs because of how bilingualism can be seen as a deficit for non-white, racialized people. These families and children are already facing such stigma and lowered expectations due to the rampant ableism in our country, that perhaps they are resisting this additional layer of multilingualism, not because they are ashamed of it, but because they want to protect their children from further stigma. I have friends who are educators themselves who have purposefully not disclosed their family's bilingualism on HLQs because they know that the system will likely test their children and perhaps identify them as an English language learner (ELL), and they do not want that for their children because they know the implications of that label. The resistance is not to bi/multilingualism, but to the stigma and inferiority attached to the label in U.S. schools (Cioè-Peña, 2017).

Families in the study were quick to share that English was the primary language that's spoken at home and that their child speaks. As mentioned above, when parents/caregivers are enrolling their children in school, they must fill out an HLQ. In the state where this study was conducted, this is a requirement. If families indicate that any language other than English is used in the home, regardless of whether the child speaks or uses that other language, they legally must go through the process of being assessed to determine whether or not they are an "English learner." For students with disabilities and nonspeaking students, this is a particular challenge because they often do not express themselves in ways that the test measures (i.e., for pre-K, they are often assessed on "speaking" and "listening"). This means that many bilingual nonspeaking children get labeled as English learners when they start school, whether or not English is their primary language. Oftentimes these children then are unable to pass "out" of English learner status, as they struggle to demonstrate the skills required on the annual English proficiency test that is then administered every year (until a child tests out of English learner status).

Lianna shared with me that they use Spanglish at home, but Ofelia shared that her communications with Lianna are primarily in English because Lianna started communicating with her in English only, so Ofelia followed her lead. Susana shared that Emmanual only speaks English and they only use English with him, but that their family also speaks Spanish, including his older brother, and they use Spanish when they don't want Emmanual to understand something. Emmanual has grandparents who primarily speak Spanish, so this is an example of children being cut off from communication with their families and communities because of assumptions about what's best for children labeled as disabled. When I asked Susana if she was given the choice of bilingual classes or services, she replied, "Um, yeah, it was always assumed that he would just be in monolingual, um, because we do speak primarily English at home." When I followed up and asked if there was anyone is his life who speaks primarily Spanish, she shared, "Yes, his grandparents speak a lot of Spanish to him. His grandmother, paternal grandmother, only speaks Spanish." I asked how that communication goes, when she speaks to him in Spanish, and she replied, "Um, he'll just say 'what?' *laughs* He'll say 'what, I don't know what she's saying.' He'll go to, you know my son will try to help and say she's saying this or that."

When she said, "my son," she was referring to her older son, Emmanual's older brother. This is contradicting information with what she shared about them only speaking English in the home, since Emmanual's older brother learned Spanish and English at home. It seems that what she meant is that they only speak English with Emmanual in the home, although Spanish is also used at home. As mentioned above, she did share that she and her husband will use Spanish if they don't want Emmanual to understand something. She also shared that she thought that he had started to comprehend more than they realized, because they would be speaking in Spanish, and he would ask questions in English related to what they were discussing in Spanish. This demonstrates two things: first, that families share their language status in different ways when talking about their children labeled as disabled, and second, that children are picking up and experiencing more bilingualism than they are being given credit for.

Below is an excerpt from the interview with Susana regarding their family's use of Spanish and Emmanual's languaging:

> Yeah, so he will be like 'What? What'd you say?' But as of late, he almost started understanding things because we'll talk in Spanish when we don't want him to understand something, for instance . . . and then he'll hear us, and like say, I'll think otherwise he's doing something and not listening, but then he'll ask a question related to what we're talking about and I'm like . . . is he understanding? But in the sense of like, grasping, I don't know to the extent, because he doesn't express it, he'll say words here and there, but it's not concrete, like a conversation or anything.

When I asked if her older son spoke Spanish with him at all, she replied, "Um, no, only when he bothers him."

Emmanual's case is also important to highlight because he was the oldest child in the study. At 9 years old, he had experienced a range of schooling and services, and had moved through a continuum of nonverbalism to vocal speech usage. Emmanual represents what many speech-language pathologists and special educators (and, oftentimes, parents and caregivers) desire and focus on for nonspeaking children: to develop their communication toward comprehensible spoken language. It is notable that none of his instruction had occurred in Spanish, despite his family being bilingual and his grandparents primarily speaking Spanish. As Susana shared, it was always assumed that the instruction would be in English because they primarily spoke English at home, but the discrepancy in the family use of Spanish with Emmanual's older brother is also important to note. This suggests that the bilingual confusion trope permeates families; it is not just that bilingual classes and services are discouraged or not offered at all, but families begin to internalize messages that bilingualism is too complicated or confusing for their nonspeaking children. Reading this through a DisCrit lens, Tenet 6 posits

> DisCrit recognizes Whiteness and ability as property and that gains for people labeled with dis/abilities have largely been made as the result of interest convergence of White, middle-class citizens. (Annamma et al., 2013, p. 60)

In Susana and Emmanual's case, as in the case of many racialized children and families, whiteness and spoken English became intertwined. The assumption projected onto the child and family by the school and medical systems was that in order for Emmanual to be as successful as possible in school, he needed to be as successful as possible at communicating within the bounds of perceived spoken English language. Emmanual was a child living a bilingual life; his parents were bilingual, his older brother was bilingual, and his grandparents primarily spoke in Spanish. However, when I asked Susana about the services he received and the messaging and options around bilingual services and classes, she said,

> . . . they told us not to use Spanish with him, they said just focus on the one language, because he was struggling, that it would just further confuse him, and so that would be the best option at the time, so then I completely stopped talking to him in Spanish. Because with my other son, for example, we spoke to him and he understands it to this day, my oldest, but Emmanual does not.

At the time of the interview, and for many years prior, Susana was a bilingual educator herself. Despite research showing that bilingualism is *not* a confusion factor for children with disabilities, the message persists that monolingual English schooling is the best, least confusing option (Cioè-Peña, 2017). When a child is part of a family that uses both languages, why in the world would we believe that it is less confusing for them to receive schooling in only one language? Why would it make more sense to provide speech language therapy in only one language? The child is being cut off from developing communication and learning in one of their languages and cut off from exploring many of the tools in their linguistic repertoire. It can be less apparent how this choice is impacting children when they are nonspeaking, like Emmanual was for much of his childhood. Because he was not expressing words in either language, it would have been difficult to ascertain how his monolingual schooling was limiting his Spanish communication. What is clear, however, from Susana and Emmanual's story, is that he began expressing himself in spoken English after several years of English language instruction. Because, as Susana pointed out, he seemed to understand his family's conversations in Spanish—despite them attempting to use it as a coded language around him—it would follow that had he received bilingual instruction, he might have begun to express himself more fully in both languages.

This connects to Fiona's experience with Hector. Hector has internalized a message that Spanish is inferior or undesirable, though it is not clear why he takes such an adamant stance. He frequently told Fiona, "No Spanish. Just English," despite his grandparents speaking only Spanish to him. Fiona got emotional voicing doubts about her choice to solely speak English with him and lamented that she hadn't done more to teach him Spanish or to use Spanish with him. While Fiona viewed it as a personal failing and/or personal decision to speak in English with Hector, it is important to recognize that a larger system is at play that renders bilingual services and programs a non-option—particularly for nonspeaking children from multilingual families.

When I asked Ofelia about the choice to use Spanish versus English in her speech therapy sessions with Niveyah, she shared the following:

> [I use] English, predominantly. I've used some Spanish because they're bilingual, pero igual. . . . I was talking to mom, the parents, and they primarily speak with her in English, they don't speak Spanish, um, and they prefer English since they at home primarily speak English. I still throw it in just because you never know if a child may understand, you know, baño instead of bathroom. Little things like that, yeah so it was more the parents who preferred the English dominant for therapy, I just for the most part just go with it . . . [Echolalia] mm, I wanna say maybe she doesn't do it as much in Spanish? Or she tries to say it in Spanish um, but but no, I'd say more in English.

She shared that even when parents tell her that English is primarily spoken at home, if she knows a family is bilingual, she'll still use both English and Spanish. She said, "English, predominantly. I've used some Spanish because they're bilingual, pero igual." This is so fascinating because she first says predominantly English, but then says they're bilingual so she also uses Spanish, *pero igual. Pero igual* literally means "but equal," which seems to imply she was using both languages equally. But if she was, as she stated, using predominantly English, then Spanish was not being used equally. This linguistic ideology is illuminating; there is a recognition of bilingualism and use of Spanish, but only as an afterthought in relation to a child or family's identity—English took predominance.

She mentioned that a child may know the word *baño* instead of bathroom, for example. This is a clear understanding of translanguaging without necessarily using the terminology for it. She also seems to indicate an understanding that even if a family shares with her that they only use English at home, their definition of using English may still include Spanish. This dynamic view of language is very critical to breaking the myth that multilingual people have two distinct linguistic repertoires.

Bilingual Nonspeaking and Minimally Speaking Children as Languaging Experts

Kaitlin, Bernardo's teacher, shared that Bernardo reacted nonvocally when the educators in the room (a) attempted to use Spanish, and/or (b) did not understand Bernardo's expression; she said that clearly Bernardo knew that their Spanish is elementary, and he reacted to it accordingly.

> You know he just gets like he'll just he'll he's kind of funny about it sometimes, 'cause you know some of us do, um, there are some words that some of us have and some of us understand, we're not billing, we're not fluent in Spanish, none of us are, in my room, but there are certain things, like I do have a little Spanish-English dictionary, um, we use that. We, um, but what he gets frustrated, it's more or less it's like comical to him in a sense. Like he'll be like more or less like okay I'm not gonna continue to try to get this person to understand what I'm trying to say. . . . And he'll have a little like smirk on his face and he'll like chuckle a little bit.

Kaitlin noted that when the teachers struggled to understand what Bernardo was expressing to them, he would smirk or make a face at them and just walk away. Despite not being able to identify what he intended to get across, Kaitlin demonstrated a deep understanding of Bernardo's intent to communicate, and even positioned him as the expert, noting that it was their shortcoming that they could not make sense of his expression, and that he recognized this dynamic as well. She embodied an asset-based lens.

Niveyah's mom Lianna shared that they used Spanglish at home. She sought out Ofelia for speech therapy because she was a bilingual provider who could work with Niveyah in both languages. While Lianna opted to do the interviews in English, she shared that Niveyah watched television shows primarily in English but played tablet games in both languages. She noted that she primarily expressed words or word approximations in English, but that she understood and responded to communication in Spanish as well as English. Another interesting dynamic that is demonstrated through Niveyah's case study is that of echolalia. While Niveyah is described by Ofelia as echolalic, meaning she repeats words or phrases that she has heard, Ofelia noted that Niveyah primarily repeated words in English. I wonder if this is due to less time spent engaging with oral language in Spanish, if the primary language that is used in the household is indeed English, or if it is because she tends to repeat things in large part from television shows, which she primarily watches in English, so is accustomed to vocally forming English words more so than Spanish ones.

Hector received one set of his early intervention services in Spanish. Fiona shared that this was just circumstantial because the speech provider was from Puerto Rico and felt more comfortable in Spanish, and asked Fiona if she would like him to do Spanish services with him. She agreed but noted that this is the only Spanish instruction he has received. His grandparents, who babysit him a lot, only speak Spanish, and it is Fiona's first language, but she noted that she and her partner only speak English with Hector. She did, however, correct herself and note that she used certain words for foods in Spanish; the translanguaging that occurred in their household was so seamless she almost forgot to mention it. She shared that she was so concerned about his language development that she stuck to English with him—a common trend and trope for parents of bilingual children newly identified with disabilities. When I asked him a question in Spanish, he said, "No Spanish. Speak English." Fiona told me that he responded this way any time that she spoke Spanish, and she felt a bit ashamed that she had not been more adamant about teaching him Spanish. When I asked if bilingual early intervention services were presented to her as an option, she said no, again citing that the only reason he received any bilingual support was because of the identity of the provider, which was coincidence. The lack of options provided to Hector and Fiona furthers the myth of bilingualism as a confusion factor for young children receiving special education and/or early intervention services. While she did not receive any explicit messaging about bilingualism being too confusing for him, the assumption that all services would proceed monolingually in English reified the notion that monolingual English services are the desirable norm for any and all children, including Hector. Fiona internalized this message, as we can see when she said that she only used English out of concern for his language development.

Bilingual Education Access, Options, and the Language of "Success"

The sun must set on the narrative that bilingualism is too confusing for children who deviate from the school and medical-prescribed norm. These norms are racist and problematic at their core, and yet the pervasive trope that any form of disability or communicative difference is indicative of a lowered capacity for multilingualism persists. Because we do not have systems in place to perceive children's full communicative intent and expression, we tend to narrow our offerings to those that fall within the scope of our narrow professional capabilities and comprehension. As it stands now, most special educators and speech-language pathologists in the United States are white, and monolingual, and English-speaking, while only 6.5% of speech-language pathologists identified as being bilingual on the American Speech–Language–Hearing Association's national survey (ASHA, 2020). This drastically limits the services that schools and providers can offer to bilingual children and families, but it does not have to limit how we train educational professionals to perceive children's communication. Resources like City University of New York–New York State Initiative on Emergent Bilinguals' "Teaching Emergent Bilinguals Even If You're Not One" (2017) provide tools for educators to begin to design their pedagogy from a place of multilingualism, regardless of the named languages spoken by the educator. Kaitlin was an example of a monolingual educator who represents a turn toward a multilingual, multimodal perception of children and their communication. While she recognized that she did not have the tools to understand Bernardo at all times, she also recognized that he was expressing himself and recognizing when his teachers had limited understanding of his expression. Rather than trying to get him to assimilate to their forms of perception, she identified the teachers' deficiencies and need for more expansive understanding.

When asked why she felt it was important for children to have access to bilingual speech-language pathologists, Ofelia, a bilingual Spanish-English speech-language pathologist herself, shared,

> It's not only about the children, it's also about the families too, because I've noticed in a lot of families that the child is bilingual, but it's monolingual English, the families prefer monolingual English, but it's only only Spanish, the house is Spanish, so I think it's more for the families. Also, I think it also goes with just a cultural competency, you I think you're a little more aware, you're relatable to certain situations, you can relate to how a child was raised, or certain things that happen in a certain Latino, Latin households, and it helps you, um, the child needs that additional support, whether it's a cultural understanding of why the child takes off their shoes in the middle, before he enters a session, very common, um, as simple as as simple as that. So while I am a bilingual SLP I think it's

> also about the whole cultural perspective of a child, and then also the cultural perspective of the family itself, so I think for that reason, not only language but holistically that is important, so you can understand the child and the family.

As Ofelia's quote emphasizes and uplifts, families have often internalized the notion that English is the language that services should be occurring in if their child is to be successful. As she also pointed out, though having a bilingual speech-language pathologist or educator is important for the bilingual development of the child, bilingualism in and of itself is not enough. Understanding the cultural context of children and families is also extremely important. When she discussed a child taking his shoes off, what she did not say but what was implied is that this cultural move is easily misunderstood as inappropriate under a white supremacist framework of appropriate cultural behaviors (Padía & Traxler, 2020). Similar to Kaitlin, she was acknowledging that multimodal semiotics interplays with multilingualism when children are engaged in meaning-making.

Hector was another example of a child growing up in a bilingual family whose access to Spanish was limited. When I asked him if anyone at school speaks Spanish, he said "Um, abuelo." Hector was a child who did not speak much at all, and even less so in Spanish, but he clearly noted that he used Spanish with his grandparents and that they speak Español to/with him. His instant recognition that Spanish is connected to abuelo means that he recognized that he lived a bilingual life and that people who were important to him in his life used Spanish, and used it with him. When I asked him if grandma spoke Español with him, he said "They speak that, I don't speak that. They just speak that. . . . Yeah, they just speak that to me."

I asked Fiona, Hector's mother, for clarification around the language(s) that various family members in Hector's life used. Knowing that his Spanish-speaking grandparents often babysat him, I asked if he ever watched Spanish television shows with them.

> Oh no, he doesn't like that. He doesn't like that and he'll actually tell them to change the channel. . . . I don't know why. I really want him to learn Spanish and everybody looks at me like 'you speak Spanish! Spanish is your first language and your child doesn't speak Spanish?' But it's like I try, and he just won't respond to me, and he'll close up. Maybe it's also on me, maybe I should speak more in Spanish, but I wish that we would've started with Spanish, 'cause eventually he will learn English in school, that's what happened with me, my first language was Spanish. . . . I don't know, maybe we do have to talk to him a little more in Spanish, even if he doesn't like it.

Children who experience bilingualism at home notice when bilingualism is absent at school, even when they are labeled with disabilities and/or do not speak to express what they notice. Kaitlin, Bernardo's teacher, mentioned that he'd get frustrated sometimes because not all the teachers are bilingual, and even those who are had difficulty understanding his vocal expression, because it was not always clearly articulated. She also clearly identified how he was aware of which adults were using Spanish correctly and which weren't. This again speaks to the notion that children live bilingual lives and are bilingual beings, regardless of whether they are expressing their bilingualism vocally. Interestingly, despite his issues with articulation, Bernardo did not have an IEP, so he was not one of the kids who received speech language pathology services, although he attended a preschool that offered inclusive education. Perhaps because this school did have children who were considered entirely nonspeaking, he was not one of the children who was identified for services. It is also relevant to note that many schools do not refer children for special education evaluation for at least 2 years—and sometimes more—if they are bilingual or if English is not their primary language. This is done to safeguard against misdiagnosis of children who are multilingual. However, many educators and caregivers are not informed that if a child is exhibiting the same language difficulties in all the languages that they speak, waiting a set period of time to evaluate them for learning supports might be detrimental to their progress. This is why it is crucial that we have bilingual providers, assessors, educators, and administrators who can support children holistically and identify whether communication is impacted in all of the languages that they use or just one. Even as we advocate for more bilingual medical and educational providers, we must also recognize that this framework of language delay is deficit-oriented and still relies on whether the children can express themselves through the typical spoken oral modality.

Kaitlin noted that Bernardo was fun to have in the classroom and that he was an asset with a good sense of humor. Her perception of him as funny, despite him not using many spoken words—or at least not ones that she could comprehend—and her assessment of his facial expressions when the teachers tried to use Spanish—indicates that Kaitlin comprehended communication beyond the spoken word. She read Bernardo as a funny kid with personality who engaged in communication despite it not being spoken English words all the time. Bernardo was a kid whose family primarily used Spanish and who attended school primarily in English. His mom noted that his expression shifted when he came home from school. She shared the anecdote introduced in Chapter 1 about him saying "*I love it patos*!" when he meant that he wanted to take off his shoes (zapatos) himself; we see here the translanguaging as he was attempting to share his thoughts and ideas using traditional oral language. His mom also said,

> It's kind of a mix, although I think something I've noticed is that like on Friday he'll come home speaking a lot of English after school and then by Sunday

> afternoon after all weekend of speaking to him in Spanish it'll be a little more Spanish, and it just kind of goes based on whatever he's been exposed to most recently.

He also demonstrated the translanguaging characteristic of using all the meaning-making skills at his disposal to get his ideas across. This is something that all people do naturally; the effectiveness of the communication depends on the perceptive capabilities of the person or people engaging with the child. In Bernardo's case, his family understood his expression, both because of their bilingualism and because they have studied and learned him. His mom shared,

> . . . The other night my husband only wanted to read him one book and of course he wanted to delay bedtime and read another book, I think he was just saying it in English because I think libro is a little hard for him because of the r . . . So he was just screaming like BOOK BOOK BOOK, um, and that's, that's pretty typical of a tantrum for him . . . Like he'll use like a word, like the word to him that symbolizes whatever the problem is, and then he'll just like scream it over and over.

One family ended up having access to both bilingual Spanish-English and American Sign Language instruction in a preschool setting by happenstance. Katherine shared that her daughter Katrina just happened to end up in a daycare that used sign language and also where the teachers were bilingual and used Spanish as well as English. She said, "It just happened to align, so I was very happy." Once she was notified by Katrina's teachers and doctor that there was cause for concern with her speech development, however, she shared that she intentionally researched bilingual speech therapists. The focus on bilingualism as a support actually demonstrates a resistance and counternarrative to the "bilingualism is too confusing" trope; Katherine recognized that if her daughter was going to be viewed as her whole self and supported holistically in her communication development, she needed the support of a bilingual speech language pathologist.

> I researched because I got like . . . I spoke to the teacher, the teacher said that she was concerned, the pediatrician was concerned, I was also concerned, so I got a referral from my pediatrician and then I researched a bilingual speech therapist, and I found her.

Katherine also noted that as Katrina's vocal vocabulary started developing, she used English most of the time but tended to use Spanish for food: "Everything else [she uses English], but for food she'll say like agua, or manzana." Katrina, along with Niveyah, was the other child in the study with whom Ofelia worked with, so she also received services in both Spanish and English. Ofelia stated that when Katrina began services with her, "There was no dominant language at the time . . . when I first started with Katrina, so I just [use] both, with her." Ofelia went on to say,

> And there was some of the situations where she catered better and understood more of the Spanish and some where she understood more of the English and when she kind of had more, developed more skills and more language and I noticed that was more English based, I would kind of reiterate what I just said in Spanish to kind of keep promoting that, because she's, um, Dominican and she would learn both languages. . . . [She responded] Mainly in English, I think the main thing that she had in Spanish was like *agua*, more like food-related things. . . . Um, but anything, you know, academic related or anything that we were doing was English.

It's difficult to know if the child gravitated toward the more "academic" things in English, or if it was the choice of the therapist to focus on academic things in English, but either way, the idea still gets reinforced that English is the language of academic and developmental success. Flores and García (2020) note the distinction between basic interpersonal communication skills (BICS) and cognitive academic language proficiency (CALP) (Cummins, 2008) by reminding us that all language is academic and to imply otherwise is to devalue certain funds of knowledge (Flores & García, 2020; González et al., 2005). The linguistic service delivery choices that happen, even in a specifically bilingual speech language pathology session, wherein the parents sought out the bilingual services and bilingual provider, reinforce the supremacy of spoken English language as the prime form of communication. A pedagogy of perception disrupts this perception of the supremacy of spoken English to truly honor the multitude of ways that people communicate.

Even when families and educational professionals might desire or recommend bilingual services or classes, access is often limited because of how few bilingual providers work for public agencies or agencies that accept insurance like Medicaid. Ofelia identified the lack of bilingual speech language pathologists available to families who use this type of insurance. When I asked how families got matched with her as a bilingual speech provider, she replied,

> I see them through insurance and I am probably the only bilingual SLP on [the system], and also the only one who's around here, so conveniently located, so it just kind of worked out that way, that I'm the only one. 'Cause I know a lot of the time I think they just do the search and kind of just, the insurance accepts the locations.

As Ofelia noted, some families ask for and prefer English as the language of instruction. It is important to place this preference in context. When affordable, convenient access is such an issue and bilingual providers and educators are so few and far between, it makes sense that families would want their children to learn in the language they are going to be subjected to in most learning spaces: English.

COMMUNICATIVE JUSTICE TAKEAWAYS

Equipped with the knowledge that families are often counseled against using bilingual services or supports or not offered them at all, because bilingualism is labeled as "too confusing" for our nonspeaking and/or disabled students, how can we as educators uplift, include, and sustain multilingualism in our classrooms? You do not need to be bilingual yourself to support students' bilingualism. In the same way that you do not need to belong to a particular ethnic group to include elements of that ethnicity in your classroom, you can incorporate multilingualism—and multimodal multilingual opportunities—into your classroom environment and practices.

Children and families should be presented with bilingual options; as teachers, we can advocate for families to know their rights and to know that they are entitled to bilingual services. Often families are counseled against this because there is a lack of educational professionals who are bilingual and can provide the service, so it becomes a choice for the caregivers of moving the child to a different school or keeping them at their familiar site with monolingual services. Supporting families in finding what works best for them, and affirming for them that bilingualism is *not* too confusing but is actually a dynamic that will help their child blossom into their full self, is important.

Some traditional neuropsychological research, premised on a medical model of disability, indicates that introducing a child to two or more languages places a heavy cognitive burden on a child labeled as disabled (Toppelberg et al., 1999). However, because all the children in this study were at least partially immersed in family settings where Spanish is the primary language (for most of the children, this was through spending consistent time with their Spanish-speaking grandparents), the children were already being exposed to multiple languages. Providing services and programming solely in English means that they are only formally being supported in developing their communication skills in English. It does not mean that they are being exposed only to English. Since they already have both languages in their cognitive and communicative repertoire, it is doing them a vast disservice when their formal educational supports are not engaging with all of the named languages that their families use.

TEACHING IN ACTION

This section offers tools to consider the various facets of power and oppression in our learning spaces, and how they relate to bilingualism and nonspeaking expression. Table 3.2 introduces the framework of the "Four I's" of Power and Oppression filled out with an example, and Table 3.3 offers a graphic organizer to analyze your own classroom and school context. To extend this beyond the classroom experience, what follows is a template for conducting ethnographic interviews with families to learn more about their own experiences with language and language access, particularly in the context of schooling and special education services. Finally, I reflect on how classroom teachers and speech therapists can collaborate to support each other's pedagogy and to ultimately support nonspeaking bilingual children as much as possible.

The Four I's of Power and Oppression: A Framework for Identifying Power and Oppression in Schools

A framework that I find particularly useful to think about power and how it plays out in our learning spaces is the Four I's of Power and Oppression (Grassroots Institute for Fundraising Training, 2012; Padía, 2020). The Four I's are: Ideological, Institutional, Interpersonal, and Internalized:

> Ideological oppression involves widespread thoughts, ideas, and beliefs that justify and uphold the oppression in question. Institutional oppression involves the policies, practices, and structures that legally prescribe and maintain the oppression in question. Interpersonal oppression is typically the easiest to identify, because it involves person-to-person interactions of discrimination that demonstrate the oppression in question. Internalized oppression defines the way that oppressed people come to believe oppressive ideological ideas about themselves. (Padía, 2020, p. 231)

I offer an example (Table 3.2) of the Four I's of Power and Oppression completed below, and then a template with questions to interrogate how WMSE shows up in your own learning spaces (Table 3.3), as well as questions for how we can reorient toward expansive communication practices and partnerships.

Ethnographic Interviewing: Family Experiences With Bilingualism and Special Education

Conducting interviews with your nonspeaking bilingual students and their families can provide insights into families' experiences with information

Table 3.2. The Four I's of Power and Oppression: English-Only Education in the United States

Issue	English-Only Education in the United States
Ideological	The ideologically oppressive element of English-only education is the notion that English is superior to all other languages. The belief that English is the best and only language that should be used in the United States, and that if you want to be American you need to learn English, underpins the concept of English-only education.
Institutional	Policies, practices, and laws that reify the supremacy of English, such as state exams that are only offered in English, college applications only being accepted in English, schools that teach limited content to English as a New Language students because of the belief that until they learn English, they are neither ready nor deserving of rigorous academic content, are all institutionally oppressive aspects of English-only education.
Interpersonal	When monolingual English-speaking students tell other students to "Go back to [insert home country here]. This is America, we speak English here," they are demonstrating an interpersonally oppressive element of the notion of English-only [education].
Internalized	When an emergent bilingual student labeled as an English learner believes that they are less intelligent than their monolingual English-speaking peers because they do not have a full grasp of the English language, they have internalized the belief that English is the superior language and that their worth is dependent on their relationship to English.

about and access to bilingual services and classes. As we saw with many of the families in this study, caregivers are often counseled against bilingual services under the framing that bilingualism is too much or too confusing for nonspeaking children and/or children with disabilities. Other families might be given the option of bilingual services or programs but faced with the reality that the only programs for their child's age/grade are far away geographically, thus placing a hardship on the family. As educators, asking families questions like the ones below can help you determine what messages and offerings families have received about language of instruction and what they desire moving forward. Even if you are not a bilingual educator yourself, you can work to incorporate multilingual, multimodal supports within your own instructional practice.

1. When was your child first identified to receive services (early intervention, special/inclusive education, any others)?

Table 3.3. The Four I's of Power and Oppression: Communicative Justice Learning Environment Evaluation

Issue	Communicative Justice
Ideological	• What ideas about how students can and should express themselves are present in our learning space (in terms of both modality and named language)? • What types of communications are considered valid, acceptable, and valuable?
Institutional	• What policies am I required to adhere to related to students' expression? What local, state, or national standards for speaking and communication are we held to? • How do we measure and assess students' knowledge? What forms of communication are accepted and/or considered when we look at what students know and how they share that knowledge? • What systems are in place in the learning environment to support students' engagement and expression? (Consider multiple modalities like auditory, physical movement, visual graphics, written words, spoken words, assistive technology and communication devices, etc.)
Interpersonal	• How do I track student progress and how is that impacted by the way they communicate and the way I communicate with/perceive them? • How are students treated who do not communicate in spoken, English language—by adults? By other children? • How do students communicate with one another? What do the forms of communication look like beyond spoken language interactions?
Internalized	• How do students feel about their ability to communicate and be understood by others? (This one may be trickier to ascertain, but it is important to keep on our radar. Tools like student self-assessments where they indicate what they learned and identify their progress toward their goals, as well as how they feel about their progress, can help us to understand their internalized ideas about their own value as it relates to how well they are understood.)

2. What language(s) were you offered for the delivery of these services?
3. What information did you receive about the language of instruction for your child?
4. What language(s) do you use at home?
5. In your ideal world, what languages would be used with your child in school and why?

Educator Team Collaborations: Speech Providers and Classroom Teachers

Finally, as educators we do our best work when we collaborate, not just with families and children, but also with one another. Teachers and speech language therapists can work together to identify practices to support student expression in and outside the classroom. Ideally, when children receive speech language services, the speech provider will *push into* the classroom, meaning they provide services to the child inside of their classroom, rather than *pulling the child out* for a separate session. This enables both the speech provider and the classroom teacher to observe each other in action with the child and to work together to share strategies for being in a communication community with our nonspeaking bilingual children. If one of the educators is bilingual and one is monolingual, the team can also share resources on how to integrate multilingualism into the communication practices used with and by the child. If neither is bilingual, the team can work together to conduct the ethnographic interview listed in the previous section, and work with the family to share home and school practices when it comes to communication—in terms of both multiple languages and multiple modalities.

CHAPTER 4

"We Make Our Own Systems"

> We make the road by walking.
>
> —Miles Horton

NONSPOKEN COMMUNICATION SYSTEMS IN THE CLASSROOM

One year, I had a minimally speaking bilingual student, Kenny, in my class who would dive under tables and furniture in the room when he was upset. Kenny was not classified as nonverbal because he would vocalize a few words or sentences from time to time, but the majority of the time he used facial expressions, gestures, and sounds other than words to communicate. At the start of the year, when he would hide under furniture, it was often unclear to me or my class aide what had upset him, and he did not use words to share; instead he would throw and kick things around the room and flop his body on the floor. It would take hours sometimes for him to be convinced to come out from under the furniture he was hiding under.

I decided to talk with him when he was not in crisis to see if we could set a plan to support him when he started to get upset. We created a hand signal together that would indicate that he was getting upset and needed my attention. We practiced using the hand signal that day; every time that he used it, I would mirror it back to him, and then come over to check on him when I was finished with the task or student at hand. I wanted to make sure he knew that the hand signal would be honored, so we reinforced it before a crisis occurred. The first time he needed to use the hand signal when he was getting upset, our plan worked perfectly. I repeated the hand signal back to him and then went over to check on him. Using a combination of spoken words in Spanish and English (mostly from me) and visuals and gestures (mostly from him), we agreed that he would go take a walk with the class aide, get some water, and return to class. He did so smoothly and returned to his work.

The second time he used the hand signal, however, was not such a success. I was in the middle of a hands-on activity with a small group doing a sink-or-float experiment. I could not step away to check on him at that moment. I acknowledged his hand signal by repeating it, but it took me 10 minutes to go over to him. He was already under an easel in the corner of the classroom by that time. Once again, it took over an hour for him to climb out from under the easel. Something more had to change. We met again to plan together and agreed that he would use a special communication notebook to draw or write his feelings if the teachers in the room were unable to check in with him right away. We designated a special drawer in the teacher desk for him to drop the notebook off when he had shared something he wanted us to read, and created another hand signal for him to use to alert us that the journal was waiting for us. Truth be told, I think he preferred that notebook to communicating vocally or gesturally with myself and the class aide. He carried that notebook with him everywhere and took great pride in sharing it with us. His notebook communication included a mix of Spanish and English written words and drawings. We found something he felt comfortable with and that enabled him to be heard in a way that worked for him—and also ensured that he knew that I was going to respond to his communication, even if I wasn't able to at the immediate moment he desired attention. The diving under furniture stopped after that. He would sometimes frown or use the hand signals repeatedly if he was not happy with how long we were taking to get to him or his notebook, but we always got to it, and he consistently used his hand signals and notebook to share his feelings with us. We made our own system based on what Kenny wanted and needed—and we made our own system to ensure that we were understanding his communication when he was unable or uninterested in using spoken words (in either formal language) to express himself.

KEY IDEA(S)

Table 4.1 offers prompts related to communication and expertise. If some of your answers included medical professionals, speech language pathologists, and/or teachers, hold that thought. If your answers included caregivers, parents, siblings, and, most importantly, the child themself, you are already on your way to implementing what I call *reciprocal carryover.* Reciprocal carryover moves us away from the idea that children are successful when strategies that are implemented by educational professionals are "carried over" at home, and suggests that children are seen as their most full selves and perceived as the most robust communicators when educators also "carry over" the communicative techniques and modalities that are used at home (Padía,

Table 4.1. Stop and Jot

Stop and Jot
Let's do a quick activity together. Take a moment and reflect on your answer to the following question:
Who is an expert on a child's communication?
Make a list of everyone that comes to mind.
Now respond to the following questions:
Who is an expert on a child's communication development? Who has the skill set necessary to support a child in developing their communication and language?
Again, make a list of everyone that comes to mind.

2023). Who is more of an expert on a child's communication than the child themself and the people who communicate with the child on a daily basis? Families are often more comprehensive perceptive partners than teachers, in part because families do not have the same investment in getting children to "master" a standardized norm or metric. Educators are evaluated on how their students progress when measured against typical developmental norms and skills that have been identified by medical professionals and educational policymakers. This impacts educators' roles as white listening subjects (Flores & Rosa, 2015); it makes sense that when you are measured—and paid—according to white culture of power norms (Delpit, 1995), you end up adhering to them. I do not write this to point the blame at educators. I was an elementary school teacher myself, and as I have shared, I unwittingly played the role of white listening subject and enforcer of problematic language norms myself at times. This chapter offers an alternative, a roadmap to unlearning our role as white listening subject, to turn toward families and children as our teachers to help us create more just communication communities in our classrooms and learning spaces. Families and children co-construct systems for languaging and communication that differ from those that are typically recognized and encouraged in formal educational spaces (Padía, 2023). Carrying families' communication practices from home and community spaces into the classroom can strengthen our teaching practice and honor and support children in a holistic way.

Families often create their own systems for ascertaining what a nonspeaking child in the family is communicating. Because their daily lives are inextricably linked, becoming effective communication partners is not an option in the same way that it might be for someone who works with the child in a professional learning space. Learning to communicate in ways that both parties perceive and feel understood is essential within family care webs. As part of their theory of crip linguistics, Henner and Robinson (2021) introduced the idea of linguistic care work:

> Linguistic care work embraces interdependence between languagers as a practice of collective access in desire to work toward mutual understanding. Working together to ensure that all languages in conversation can make themselves understood, and be understood in kind is linguistic care work. (p. 6)

Family systems of care include linguistic care work; the work and care that go into understanding one another's communication is something that educators can learn from and integrate into the classroom community. Turning toward reciprocal carryover invites us to consider our own perceptive shortcomings and growth areas. We can learn from nonspeaking young children and their families' communicative systems to turn away from the question "What is the child not yet able to express?" and instead ask ourselves, "What am I not yet able to perceive?"

Two key concepts that I explore in this chapter are *communication communities* and a *pedagogy of perception.* I use the term *communication communities* to describe the classroom as a space where we interact and exchange ideas with one another when we become a communication community. A communication community is based on shared understandings of what "counts" as communication and how we engage with one another through a range of modalities, including but not limited to spoken words, written words, other visuals, gestures, body language, eye gaze, role play, technology, and more. When we embrace a wide range of forms of communication, we ensure that all individuals are included and valued within our community. When certain forms of communication are acknowledged and others are not, we send the message that only people who communicate in a certain way are central or valuable members of our learning community. An inclusive, just communication community is premised on the idea that we always strive to be the best perceptive partners possible to one another—to meet one another in navigating and perceiving the various forms of communication that we each use to do our best to understand one another.

This perceptive partnership that strengthens our communication communities can be supported through what I call a *pedagogy of perception.* I use pedagogy of perception to describe classroom teaching that encourages the development of communication communities that recognize, respond to, and honor as many forms of communication and expression as possible for the sake of understanding one another. Through a pedagogy of perception, not only can we work on not just perceiving our individual students' perceptions from the standpoint of the teacher, but as teachers, we can also work to learn from how children interact with one another and support them in their engagement with one another as part of a loving, inclusive communication community.

THE STATUS QUO: PROBLEMATIC CURRENT PRACTICES

Families and children themselves are not considered experts in their own communication and development; school and medical "professionals" are positioned as the ones with the knowledge and qualifications to "help" children develop their communication and/or communicate "better" (i.e., in spoken, standardized English). The extent to which teachers and related service providers often learn from and about families sometimes begins and ends with family questionnaires sent home at the beginning of the year. These questionnaires often ask questions about the child's interests, hobbies, allergies, and any other information that the parents or guardians would like to share. While this information is important, it does not even begin to paint a picture of who a child is. When it comes to our bilingual nonspeaking students, the types of questions that we ask families must go so much deeper and be so much more involved. If a family has created a system of communication that enables them to perceive when their nonspeaking bilingual child is upset, when they are requesting an item, when they are sharing joy, when they are hungry, and so forth, that system is crucial information for classroom teachers and school professionals to learn about. This is not the type of information that we will learn from families on a typical back-to-school family questionnaire.

Families like the ones in this study did not even think to share the systems they had created with their child's educators because they did not realize that they had created innovative, powerful systems of communication that could be useful in schools. Whether or not we mean to, as educators we often uphold the notion that the expertise on communication development comes from those of us with professional training and degrees. We do this by not asking families about the communication systems they use. We do this by not realizing that we have so much to learn from families—and from nonspeaking bilingual children themselves. This is an ideological problem, not a personal one. This is a problem in the way that we are trained as professionals. Even those of us, like myself, who began our teaching careers with a deep commitment to children and families' expertise are not taught how to inquire about said expertise. If we don't know the questions to ask, it is unlikely we will ever find the answers. Toward the end of this chapter, in the Teaching in Action section, we will revisit this notion and discuss strategies for eliciting this knowledge and expertise from families in order to integrate it into classroom practice.

LEARNINGS FROM CHILDREN, FAMILIES, AND EDUCATORS

Here we will use case studies of families who created systems for communication and mutual perception beyond the scope of the recommendations made to them by educational professionals. The nonspeaking or minimally speaking bilingual children were receiving early intervention and/or special education services that included speech language therapy, and yet these families relied on systems to understand each other that were outside of the orbit of "expertise" that was presented to them by the medical and educational professionals who worked with the children. The families had not shared their systems with the service providers. They did not talk about their family language systems as strategies to support their child's communication development. Rather, they were thoughtful about their *own* communication as adults and caregivers. All of these systems were shared when I asked them, "What helps you understand your child?" While it is true that my question removed the focus on the child's languaging and left it open, it is important to note that all of the caregivers responded with a focus on what they had done or needed to do to be in a communication community with their children, rather than identifying what their children needed to do to be in communication community with them.

Multimodal, Multisensory Systems of Communication

Niveyah, at 4 years old, was not expressing herself with vocal speech except for repeating words or phrases people said to her or from her favorite TV shows and movies. Her mother, Lianna, shared that she turned requesting into a game at home, to ensure that Niveyah never felt bad for communicating without words. She would ask Niveyah what the color of her desired item was when Niveyah made a sound that the family recognized to mean she wanted something; Lianna would go down a list of colors in both Spanish and English and Niveyah would shake or nod her head to indicate the corresponding color. Lianna also said that she would always respond to Niveyah's sounds, even if she had no idea what she was saying, because she recognized that her daughter was communicating with her when she made sounds; even if she did not fully understand, she was intent on affirming her daughter's role as a communication partner within their family. When I observed Niveyah and her sisters playing together at a park, I saw another system of communication that the sisters had constructed together. One of the older sisters tapped my arm and said, "Watch this!" She then called Niveyah's name. Niveyah made a sound that was not discernable as a word, something like "*ahummm.*" Her sister then repeated the same sound Niveyah had made, "*ahummm*," pointed to me, said "Lilly," and then repeated the sound again, "*ahummm.*" Her sister then pointed at me again and looked at Niveyah. Niveyah followed her sister's gesture, looked at me, and said, "Lilly." Her sister smiled and ran off to go down the slide. These young people had developed a system wherein the sisters who did use spoken words incorporated Niveyah's sounds and vocalizations into their own vocabulary and used them to help their little sister learn spoken words. This recognition that Niveyah's communication had value, even though she did not use identifiable words, speaks to the ways families create systems of affirmation, inclusion, and belonging.

Susana said that when her son Emmanual was younger and only had about five to 10 words that he orally articulated, he would use a lot of sounds and "He would point a lot and push me, or, you know, like grab my hand and take me to what he wanted." Here Susana explained that though Emmanual did not use words, and it was harder for her to determine what he wanted, they had a system that they used to ensure that he was understood in the best way possible. This system included pointing and physical movement, both him urging her toward things and him leading her to them. She also explained that Emmanual had intensive behavioral issues and had early intervention supports for them until he was around 5 years old, at which point they stopped because they were able to figure out a system to understand him better.

> . . . the behavior was a result of us not understanding him . . . and once we developed a system . . . that behavior stopped. . . . . He just would go on a whole like tantrum, you know, like he would go off running and throw things and do things just to get our attention. 'Cause I didn't understand what he was saying.

Susana went on to say that despite Emmanual never being classified with autism,

> One pathologist told me he did fit like on the spectrum, so with him, like for instance, um, his behavior's due to, um, multiple things, like it could just be from being tired, so keeping a routine is essential for him, it, um, a daily routine, like if any change, he does not do well. So knowing things that he's used to doing, I try to maintain that same schedule. On the weekends he has a different schedule, but he know he has to go to games, he has to do X, Y, Z, but it's like any time he has a little free time, it's like a little bit of crazy comes out.

For Susana and Emmanual, finding a routine helped both of them understand what to expect, and it also helped Susana feel she better understood Emmanual's wants and needs. She read his decrease in frustration and tantrums as communication that he was more at ease and content with the routines they set up together. Susana's comment about Emmanual's behavior stopping once they developed a system mirrors what I experienced with Kenny in my own classroom. Once we had a system that ensured Kenny was understood, the behaviors of hiding under furniture and flopping on the floor subsided. A theory of reciprocal carryover would urge us as educators to engage in ongoing conversations, as well as ethnographic interviews that go beyond the start-of-year surveys teachers send home, to get a clearer picture of the types of communication partnerships that happen at home, including, but not limited to, expressions of intense emotions like joy or, in the case Susana described, frustration. Learning how families navigate these moments of communication together is invaluable to cultivating a pedagogy of perception.

Fiona was another mother who was committed to modeling sentence starters for her son Hector, particularly about the way he felt. She prompted him with a vocal, "That makes me feel . . ." when I asked how he felt about something. He replied, "No, that that that," and she prompted him again with "that makes me feel . . ." and then he said "That makes that makes me mad." When he mentioned that he got in trouble at school and threw a chicken nugget, Fiona asked, "And how did you feel?" She was working with him to express and vocalize his emotions. She mentioned that her parents, who were initially resistant to his disability diagnosis and in denial about it, had begun to take advice from her on how to work with him. Her parents, Hector's *abuelos*, would model these same sentence prompts with him in Spanish when he was at their house. Despite the resistance to Spanish that Hector showed at times (as mentioned in Chapter 3), he was being raised bilingually by multiple generations who were creating systems of communication to support them to the best of their abilities. He was an instance of a child whose spoken language developed as he got older. Additionally, when I asked him a question during our interview, Fiona repeated the same question. This may be in part because he understood her intonation and vocalization more than mine, but I also took that as her modeling for me that she asked him questions multiple times to help him process and understand. When I asked him "Does dad speak Español?" he did not answer me. She repeated the question, "Does dad speak Español?" to which he replied, "No he, no he didn't."

Her modeling of the practices that she used is something that could be carried over into school settings. Conducting observations and spending time with the child and his caregiver allowed me this window into their communication systems. As a researcher and educational professional, I would not typically have the luxury of witnessing those interactions. Those are also interactions that are so commonplace for most families, they do not think to share them on parent/caregiver questionnaires or surveys. Additionally, if teachers were working with a child like Hector to communicate in a different way, it would be helpful for both Fiona and the teachers to know which practices were used to get to a place of alignment to best support him in a holistic way.

Fiona shared how she was intentional about observing and understanding her son Hector's frustrations as forms of communication; she recognized certain facial expressions and body movements that indicated frustration arose in response to very particular sensory experiences. As recounted in Padía (2023), Fiona shared that she paid close attention to her child and the details that interested him. When he was a bit younger, she was able to identify what was bothering him when he would start to have a tantrum, despite him being nonspeaking and unable to share vocally. She shared one example of how she paid attention to the type of wheels on a toy car that Hector liked; he refused to play with toy cars with plastic wheels and would only play with rubber-wheeled cars. One day they went to a toy store, and Hector began to scream and kick on the ground after she handed him a toy car off the shelf. She was confused because the car had a rubber wheel, which she had made sure of before passing it to him. After assessing the environment, she realized that the rubber had begun to separate from the wheel's rim, and this slight difference from what he was used to was setting him off. These types of observations demonstrate deep care, love, and attentiveness. These types of observations that families make can help educators to better understand nonspeaking bilingual children like Hector. Had I known what I know now when I was Kenny's teacher, I would have talked to his parents and caregivers. I might have saved weeks of Kenny hiding under furniture if I had learned from his family about what helped them understand him and learned to apply their systems to my classroom. Kenny and I invented our own system, but perhaps we did not have to. Perhaps his family already had a system in place that I could have carried over into the classroom. These systems and observations from families do not just help us learn about how to manage problems with children; they help us learn how to recognize and honor children's joy, too.

In addition to facial expressions and bodily reactions to sensory experiences, caregivers like Fiona highlighted observing the way that they perceived echolalia (the repeating of words) as the child communicating something through the content that was being repeated. For example, Fiona suggested that phrases from TV shows that her son repeated might be another form of expression and expansive communication. Rather than writing off echolalia as intention-less communication, we can pay attention to it to see how the children are using repeated phrases to express and make sense of their own experiences.

> But yeah, like even if he's copying it off a TV show, that he's applying it to like real-life situations. So he actually does know what that means. . . . but yeah, a lot of it definitely comes from TV.

Here, we see her trying to get information from him regarding what happened during his day at school and recognizing that he was repeating phrases from shows he had watched. Ascertaining whether he was repeating these phrases to help him explain his own experience or if he was just repeating them, is something that can be uncovered if parents/caregivers and teachers work together and communicate regularly. With children like Niveyah, who echo words in multiple languages, it is important to have educators who recognize all the languages a child uses to try to determine if the echolalia might be shedding light on a particular emotion or event. When this is not possible—as is often the case in schools—recording children's conversations throughout the day and sharing them with family members can help ascertain the meaning of the echoed language. We will expand on this more in the Teaching in Action section at the end of this chapter.

Fiona also mentioned that when Hector rocked his body, she knew that he was upset and she would spend hours trying to figure out what was going on and what he was expressing. She shared that she used an Antecedent-Behavior-Consequence (ABC) chart to help her identify what was occurring in the environment that set him off. An ABC chart is a tool that is used to identify not only a behavior that a child exhibits, but what conditions were present when the behavior began, what behavior occurred, what the response to the behavior was, and what the duration and intensity of the behavior were. It is often used when students are considered to have behaviors that interrupt either their own learning, the learning of others in the classroom, or both.

> Um, a lot of it like I don't know, I'm his mom so it's just kinda like one of those things, but I don't know, I'm very, I try to be very observant with everything that he needed, um, with um, I don't know it's like, for example, I knew that when he was stressed out, he would do like, he would rock his body, so I know like okay you're stressed out, so what's stressing you out? So I know like I have to look for it, um, and I, when I used to work at [Name of place] we used to learn also about the ABC sequence. Have you heard of that? . . . So a lot of it just kinda took like my time, like just to sit there and actually like dedicate a few hours of the day to like figure out how can we help you? What's causing this? What's doing that? Also like um, um, I would just observe his behaviors for everything. Even with like a random stranger came into the house, an exterminator, anything, I would like try to see like what's his reaction.

When I asked Bernardo during one of our video calls if he had a favorite book that he liked to read with mami and papi, and then rephrased "¿Tienes un libro favorito?" he walked away from the screen. Someone who did not know the child, or even someone who did but did not understand his form of communicating, might interpret that as rudeness, disengagement, or lack of comprehension. But Florence knew that was his unspoken response to the question—and she translated for me by narrating, "Oh, he's going to get it. Okay, busca tu libro favorito!" This is an example of me, as an educational professional, needing to expand my perceptive repertoire to include actions in response to questions. Just because a child is not giving a vocal response does not mean they are not engaging with your question; in this case, Bernardo was going to locate and show me the book in response to my question. He was also specifically responding to the question in Spanish. Asking our bilingual nonspeaking children questions in all the languages they use, and then giving space for them to respond in a range of different modalities, is key to creating expansive systems of communication in our classrooms.

Independence vs. Adult Support at Home and School

Fiona also talked about enabling her child with too much prompting versus supporting him in doing tasks himself, a commitment that is important for schools and families to be on the same page about. Students often get IEP goals of independence, and independence is something pushed in terms of academic skills, but it is just as important for schools to know which tasks families are working on for independence at home. For example, if a family is working on a child being able to tie their own shoes but the teachers and class aides always tie the child's shoes for them, this is a misalignment that needs attention. Languaging isn't just about spoken words; if kids are expressing frustration with a task like buttoning their jacket or putting a block tower back together when it falls over, the act of processing the frustration and then engaging in reassembly of the item is also an act of communication—and knowing the procedure at home is important to carry over that work toward independence in the classroom/formal learning spaces. Fiona said,

> I'll even tell him like, hey, my hands are hurting, I can't help you. So then he'll try to do it. But he'll still get frustrated. So whenever he needed something back then, um, he would just cry and I would just have to figure it out.

She described that her son would cry and he didn't have the words to vocalize what was going on, so she relied on her knowledge of him, his facial expressions, and his eye gaze to figure out what he was experiencing, just as she did with the toy car in the store.

Fiona disrupted the notion that only the professionals were the experts on child development and delays when she described how faithfully she followed her gut regarding what worked for her son. She pursued her concerns about her child's development, despite his pediatrician telling her that there was nothing to worry about and refusing to write a referral for him. She called 311 herself and they responded and gave her the information and support that she needed to start the process of early intervention.

> So they came over and right then and there it was like there was no doubt. I saw everyone who would come, the occupational therapist, the speech therapist, the teacher, the psychologist—I saw everyone's reaction, like, mm, okay he wasn't doing this, or like immature play where they would give him a car, he would turn it around and just spin the wheels, and kind of like space out, spin the wheels.

She recognized the expertise that she held as Hector's caregiver, but she also recognized that she could not successfully support him alone. She noted that it takes a community of people working in alignment to best support a child like her son. This note highlights the need for reciprocal carryover, wherein formal educators are learning from caregivers in a reciprocal partnership, across all the spaces that the child experiences.

> And then the big thing is that if you're the only one doing it, it's not going to help. You need your whole family, or whoever's watching, daycare, or wherever, to also do that. . . . obviously no one's gonna do it as much as mom . . .
>
> But at least you tell them "Hey, I would like for you to do this, I need you to do it at least one, two, three times," and at least they're seeing it . . . Outside of mom. So it's a lot, I would do that a lot. And then dad also picked up on it, and he would do it all day with him, like [prompting for] help, and he's like "[Hector], I can't help unless you tell me what you want" and so then [Hector will] start saying "help, help." And then we'll know that that's how he wants to get our attention.

When Fiona said "no one's gonna do it as much as mom," she was asserting her expertise and mastery of support for her son. Miguel and Padía (in press) discuss LatDisCrit Dual Socialization (LDS), wherein families have strengths-based perceptions of and approaches to their children in their family ecosystems, but oftentimes lean on deficit frames to identify what is "wrong" with their child when working with school professionals, to ensure that their child receives as many services and supports as possible. Fiona embodied LDS when she asserted her expertise and also her belief in her son's ability to progress and develop, while simultaneously doing everything in her power to ensure he was diagnosed and pathologized according to what he could *not* yet do, in order to receive as many special education–related services as possible.

Technology as Advancement and Deterrent to Communication With Others

Families' fears and resistance regarding disability diagnosis play a role in how and when children access special education services and support.

When children are both nonspeaking and bilingual, families often fear double stigmatization. One mother of a nonspeaking bilingual child in my first kindergarten class asked me, "So when is my child going to be normal?" That same year, another mother asked me in Spanish what she did wrong to bring this (this being nonspeaking) on her son. Fiona mentioned that she knew her son needed additional support from a young age, but the rest of her family was in denial. She noted that his language regressed when he spent lots of time on a tablet, which is something that happened a lot when he spent time with other family members like his grandparents. This is another part of why it's so important to have conversations across spaces, because technology is often leveraged as a learning support for nonspeaking children. But in Hector's case, Fiona observed that he did better with expressing himself in a way that others understood when he had more limited access to technology. In this case, the child tended to turn inward when he used devices for long periods of time. This is not to say that this internal turn is bad, but in terms of supporting him in expressing himself outwardly with others, this is an important lesson to learn from caregivers regarding the interaction between technology and communication partnerships at home. Fiona shared,

> . . . and so that would also affect his communication, because he was too busy, like concentrating on, like all these things going on, that he wouldn't even care to talk.

While it may not be that he didn't "care" to talk, it certainly seems that use of technology impacted his communication with others in his life. Once Hector's grandparents started modeling the sentence prompts and conversation starters in Spanish that Fiona used with him in English, she noted that he started communicating more with other people and focusing less on his tablet.

Niveyah, for example, had a different relationship with technology. Lianna indicated that Niveyah spent time on her tablet playing educational games (both reading and math) in English and Spanish, and that Lianna and Niveyah's sisters would then quiz her on the information she learned from the tablet games and she would be able to respond to them with the correct answers. Again, every child's experience will be different. For Niveyah, it seems that use of the tablet and technology supported her ability to communicate in ways that others were more readily able to perceive and supported her process of engagement with her family. These two different engagements with technology highlight all the more the need for reciprocal carryover and transparent, ongoing communication between educators and caregivers to identify the best learning tools and supports for each child across different social environments.

Ascertaining What Happened at School Throughout the Day

Susana, during her interview, was able to call Emmanual over to ask him to clarify what services he gets on a regular basis. Because Emmanual is a child who had begun expressing himself with oral speech, he was able to tell her with words that he was not receiving occupational therapy (OT), to which she replied, "You're supposed to get it every year. But that's okay, mommy will call." Fiona expressed her fear that she would not have a full picture of what was occurring in Hector's schooling experience because he was unable to vocally explain to her. It is imperative that educators and caregivers build systems of communication and trust with one another—and with the child, as much as possible—to work together to create a full picture of what is occurring. Too often caregivers are put in a position of having to do detective work to figure out if their child is receiving what they are entitled to receive. Often, educators are wary of sharing if a school is not in compliance for fear of backlash from their administration, but it is our duty as educators to work collaboratively with families to ensure they get what they need and deserve in their learning experience.

As mentioned above, Fiona referenced using Hector's echolalia and repeating of TV show phrases to figure out what he felt about the day at school. She would pay attention to the emotions references in the scenes he repeated from his favorite shows to look for indications of his emotional state throughout the day. She also said that one day he got hurt and all he could tell her over and over was "I was sad. I was sad." So she talked to the school, and while none of them had witnessed what occurred, they had cameras and video footage. This is one way that the experiences of children might be captured, especially for students who are unable to express themselves vocally to recount what occurred during the day; it is a way for both caregivers and educators to capture, view, and work to better understand the expressions of a child. Fiona expressed concern that he won't be able to tell her what happened during the day and what went wrong. She worries about him at school because of this, and that's a major goal for her with his communication. She expressed frustration that if she doesn't explicitly ask about his day and how he did, they don't tell her:

> Because if it is then we'll correct it here at home, 'cause with me he doesn't do it. But then I asked them like, hey, did he participate today and they're like no, he didn't, um, like we don't want to force him, he didn't want to join, we asked him one time and he didn't want to and then that was that. But then it's like I kinda get upset, like if I don't ask, they don't tell.

As Fiona noted, they had video footage that she was able to review, though she had to ask for it, rather than it being offered. Cameras/video can capture body movements, facial expressions, gestures, eye gaze, and so forth that can help us become better perceptive partners, and help us learn from moments that children are unable to recount orally. Although there is often a fear of videotaping because it has insidious implications in terms of surveillance, when used as a collaborative tool, it can become part of the communication care web surrounding nonspeaking bilingual children.

Kayla, Hector's provider, said that "Mom was on point and tried everything that I suggested." But what if we exchanged roles? The whole idea behind reciprocal carryover is that we do not just expect parents and caregivers to implement what's happening in schools or service provider sessions, but that we also integrate what's happening at home into our work in formal learning spaces. Kayla also said,

> Even though I saw you the day before, things change. So how was his night? What did you do? Did he say anything? How was his morning? And I would kind of just go through this whole big thing and I would be like okay, and I would just start my session with the parents.

Kayla went on to say that she made recommendations and shared all her noticings with the parents. While this does imply that she assumed the role of "expert," sharing suggestions as the trained professional, it is also important to note that she did start her sessions with asking the parents for context. She stated that every day is a new day and there might be more information for her to learn from the family from one day to the next. While she was not asking Fiona and Hector's father for advice or recommendations on what to do during her sessions—questions that might help strengthen her practice as an educator—she was asking them for information that might help guide her sessions.

Children Have Their Own Ways of Knowing Each Other

Like Bernardo's teacher Kaitlin said and as we saw with Niveyah and her sisters, "Children have their own ways of knowing each other." Kaitlin also explained that there are ways that children communicate with one another that are beyond the bounds of spoken language:

> And you know kids, kids have their own way of communicating too, and it's not always necessarily verbally, you know what I'm saying? . . . . They kinda do naturally, they kinda know sometimes you know when they're playing with each other for, and kinda have been with each other for a long time, they kinda get a feel and they just know, you know, about the other person, and it just kinda happens. It's a natural, you know, kind of thing. . . . It doesn't involve words and language.

She expressed a view that many early childhood educators hold, that children have their own ways of meaning-making that sometimes fall outside the bounds of what adults consider to be functional communication. Without using the explicit terminology, her stance acknowledges that multimodal semiotics have an active role in children's communication whether or not the adults in a space recognize them, and that the adult white listening subject often does not have the tools to perceive communication beyond the spoken English word. Kaitlin's stance also recognizes that voices that are typically silenced and/or unheard—in this case those of children, including multilingual nonspeaking children—dialogue with one another beyond spoken language and beyond the perception of adults who primarily rely on spoken words to communicate.

Fiona talked about Hector's friend who acts as an interlocutor, communicating vocally to Fiona what happened throughout their day together. This friend is bilingual himself, and she shared that she had observed him using both languages with Hector. Fiona said,

> There are certain moments where I feel like he's not engaging with his peers in the way he should be. So, um, he definitely needs assistance with that, and that's something else that the teacher did mention, but you know his best friend's name is Edmund, Edmund loves him, and always tells me like today Hector did this, and did that, and I helped him to do this, so I'm thankful that he has a little friend that looks out for him. . . . he even tells me everything, he kinda knows how I am already, so he tells me so Hector did this today, and I helped him with this and this and that. So that's really nice. But that's also my fear. Because not everybody's that nice. And he LOVES Edmund . . . but I'm scared that when he actually goes to kindergarten, and somebody just doesn't treat him the way that he likes, it's like how is he going to react?

Regarding children's relationships and forms of communication beyond the adult gaze, Emmanual's teacher Marilyn said that he was always sitting with and helping another child in the special education resource room. When I asked if there were any nonverbal or minimally verbal kids in the class, she replied,

> I have one, he's minimally verbal. He comes from the autism room . . . That's the one that Emmanual's always helping . . . Which is interesting now that you brought that connection to my attention. He's ALWAYS helping him. I mean I think it's the fact that he's close proximity, he sits right next to him, but I have been noticing that he is always helping him.

This relationship between Emmanual and the other child who didn't speak much was one that Marilyn didn't notice because, as she noted at the start of her interview, she did not know Emmanual when he did not speak. The entire duration of her time with him, he has spoken a lot—too much, she added, laughing. During our interview, she realized that Emmanual is constantly helping his classmate who does not speak much. This is an example of children having their own ways of knowing each other and their own systems of communication. Despite the teacher's lack of awareness of their connection, Emmanual, a child who did not speak for most of his life, aligned himself with the other minimal speaker in the room. This sign of solidarity is an important, albeit quiet and subtle, act. Emmanual was subverting the stigmas of nonspeaking communication and aligning himself with a peer whom he recognized as a whole human being, who just happened to communicate differently than the status quo. Marilyn's note that Emmanual was always helping his classmate is interesting; I wonder if she perceived this to be the case because he was so verbose and his classmate was not. Perhaps her perceptive pedagogy was not yet developed enough to observe the reciprocity of the relationship. It may be that Emmanual was primarily helping his peer, but until we as educators develop a pedagogy of perception that permits us space to read all communicative acts, both spoken and unspoken, we cannot paint a complete picture of the communicative practices and relationships that occur in our classrooms. When children are young and do not yet write or type, it can be more difficult to ascertain how their bilingualism fits into their nonspoken communication. As we saw with Kenny, as kids get older, if they are given instruction in all the languages that they use, they may begin to express themselves in unspoken ways, like journal entries, in a mix of multiple languages. Part of our work as educators is to ensure we create multilingual, multimodal lessons, learning spaces, and opportunities for expression, so that our students have as many tools as possible at their disposal to communicate with one another—not just with us as adults and teachers.

COMMUNICATIVE JUSTICE TAKEAWAYS

Families and children have robust communication systems that we can and should learn from as teachers. As we saw with the caregivers highlighted in this chapter, families have a great deal of insight to offer educators about what works best with their children and how their children communicate. We must create systems of communication with families to ensure ongoing dialogue to learn from not just the young children themselves (though that is paramount), but from the families of the young children we work with. We must also do our part to engage in thorough and thoughtful observation of our students within their peer, family, and other naturalistic contexts.

Engaging in *reciprocal carryover* supports communicative justice in the classroom. The current trend is for educational professionals to share recommendations with caregivers about how to best support their child. While it is true that there is information these professionals have been trained to know and enact, it is also true that families have unique expertise and deep insight into the interests, aversions, preferences, joys, and communicative indicators of their nonspeaking bilingual children. Educators should certainly share best practices with caregivers but should also recognize that there are best practices not yet on educators' radars that they can and should be learning from caregivers and incorporating into their classroom practice.

A *pedagogy of perception* helps us be better perceptive partners within our classroom communication communities. As I mentioned earlier in the chapter, a pedagogy of perception refers to classroom teaching that encourages the development of communication communities that recognize, respond to, and honor as many forms of communication and expression as possible for the sake of understanding one another. Through a pedagogy of perception, not only can we work on not perceiving our individual students' perceptions just from the standpoint of the teacher, but as teachers we can also work to learn from how children communicate with one another and support them in their communication with one another as part of a loving, inclusive communication community.

Communication communities help us become better communication partners. Conceptualizing our classrooms as communication communities can move us toward a space where we not only honor all forms of expression, but as teachers we position ourselves as members of a community who are learning from our students, not just instructing them. We often think of communication in terms of receptive and expressive skills that live within an individual. We look at how well a student can express themself in white mainstream spoken or written English and how they comprehend information presented to them in white mainstream spoken or written English. Moving away from these standardized, narrow metrics of expressive and receptive language reorients us toward expansive communication that includes multiple modalities, named languages, dialects, and forms of expression that we can use to share ideas in our classroom communities.

TEACHING IN ACTION

We return to the idea of using video in service of collaboration here with the Shared Video Reflection Protocol. This is meant to encourage collaboration between families and educators in a way that sharing student work products cannot capture. This protocol offers new possibilities for parent–teacher/family–teacher conferences, with the aim of honoring the full communication of bilingual nonspeaking children and learning from the communication systems and analyses of the children's families. The following reciprocal carryover strategies offer pathways for teachers and educational professionals to ask the types of questions of families that will help us learn as much as possible about what occurs at home, and how we can uplift the home practices in the classroom. Finally, Tables 4.1 and 4.2 provide opportunities to build on the SIP protocol from Chapter 1; these tables offer protocols for reviewing students' accommodations with them from their IEPs, helping students learn to ask and advocate for their accommodations if they are not receiving them, and analyzing which accommodations they are finding useful, and in what ways. All of these protocols are presented here in English but are encouraged to be used in the students' and families' preferred languages when they are implemented.

Rethinking Parent-Teacher Conference Artifacts: Shared Video Reflection Protocol

Parent–teacher conferences often use artifacts like standardized and benchmark assessments and portfolios with student work products to guide the discussion on student progress. I offer a protocol for teachers and caregivers to collectively analyze video recordings of a child engaging in classroom activities with their peers and their educators. This protocol allows for multimodal, unspoken engagement to be captured and provides opportunities for caregivers to share their expertise related to certain facial expressions or bodily movements. For example, one caregiver told me that she knew her son was a few seconds away from a meltdown when he repeatedly looked upward and rocked back and forth a bit; this was a sign, she shared, that he was overstimulated and needed a quiet, dark space to help him regulate himself. This is something that the teacher did not know; sharing this information together could lead to increased support to meet the child's access and learning needs and also help teachers be better perceptive partners by learning from the perceptive communication expertise of a child's family members. When I shared this practice of collaborative video analysis with a friend of mine, she shared that she would love for her young son's teachers to engage her in this practice, since there is so much that can't be captured or that may be misinterpreted in a written update, report, or communication log. There is so much opportunity for building trust and sharing knowledge of the child through a protocol like this, to learn from the child's actions themselves, rather than just adult interpretation of actions that have been recorded in artifacts like anecdotal notes or work products. If a child rips up their paper instead of completing a drawing, for example, a video could provide insight into the facial expressions and body movements of the child, as well as their position in relation to certain objects, people, and sensory factors in the room. If we just used the artifact, the only story would be the torn-up paper.

Shared Video Reflection Protocol

1. Obtain required consent for video recording from caregivers of students in your classroom (confirm your school, organization, and/or district's requirements).
2. Identify at least two video clips, one that demonstrates engagement that you are very excited about and proud of from the child and one that you are confused about or unsure how to interpret.
3. During caregiver–teacher conferences, watch the videos together. Using low-inference notes, share what you notice in each video and ask the caregivers to identify what they notice, both in terms of the child and in terms of what is occurring in the learning environment around them. Share that this step is just to identify together the actions of the child; you are not yet interpreting the actions and environmental conditions.
4. Collectively identify what seems to work well for the child's learning in the video and what seems to be a challenge.
5. Discuss together any suggestions for how to adjust the learning environment and/or how to better perceive the child's nonspoken expression in the classroom. Be very clear that this is not about "fixing" the child, but about fixing the learning environment and transforming the classroom community to support the child's learning.
6. Identify next steps for adjusting the classroom environment and pedagogy and set a date to discuss the progress of the child in light of the adjustments. Be sure to capture recordings as you implement these changes in the classroom to discuss at your next meeting.
7. Ask caregivers if there is anything else they would like you to know about how their child communicates and learns, and anything they would recommend that you try in the classroom to help their child learn best.

Reciprocal Carryover Strategies (Adapted From Padía, 2023)

1. Ethnographic Interviewing

Based on what you know about your students and families, develop a personalized set of interview questions that you can ask families to go beyond the typical beginning-of-the-year questionnaire. These questions help paint a picture of the rich languaging landscape that families engage in—particularly for nonspeaking bilingual young children who in addition to using communication beyond spoken language, may communicate in language(s) not spoken by the educators.

Sample questions might include the following:

- How do you know when your child wants something?
- How do they communicate their wants and needs to you?
- How does your child express emotions (i.e., when they are happy, sad, frustrated, bored)?
- How do you communicate with your child when you want them to do a certain task? How do you know whether they have understood you?
- What has helped them to learn and/or communicate best in the past? Have they received any services or educational supports prior to this?

2. Family Observations

If possible, arrange to spend time with the child and their family at least once. If not possible, ask if families feel comfortable recording a mealtime or a bedtime or morning routine, so you can get a sense of how their communication occurs. There may be communication strategies that are occurring that have become so second nature for families that they would not think to report this to you as a languaging practice.

If the families feel uncomfortable recording or if you are unable to meet them outside of school, offer times that they can come spend time together at school. Setting up games on a playground or in a classroom or office space can give an opportunity for families to feel more comfortable and welcomed in the formal learning spaces, as well as a chance for you to observe the family's communication practices and habits with one another. If you do spend time observing families, be sure to write ethnographic field notes (Emerson et al., 2011) immediately after capturing all your noticings. This will ensure that your memory of the observation is distorted as little as possible while the observations are fresh in your mind. Afterward you can revisit the notes to identify practices and interactions that you can incorporate into your own pedagogy.

3. Multidirectional Communication Logs

This may sound simple, but oftentimes educators send home daily or weekly reports summarizing how children behaved and what occurred/was worked on/was learned during the school day or therapy session. Setting up a system wherein families and educators alike share daily or regular updates can yield surprising results. Any update log should also include the young person themselves. Designing the update log with a space for the child to self-assess and/or to share information with caregivers and educators is a step in involving young people in their education in a meaningful way. For some children this may take the form of pictures, while for some it may be written words. Some parents/caregivers may prefer to communicate auditorily, so building in the option of a communication log that takes the form of voice notes or video messages on a platform like Flipgrid (a site that is now retired but had video recording capabilities akin to sites like Mirror, Gravity, and Padlet) can ensure that all families are able to engage in this multidirectional communication in a way they feel most comfortable.

As you build on whatever existing communication log or structure you already have, add in things for both/all parties to share. Sample topics might include the following:

- How they communicated what they wanted to eat
- What the toileting schedule was like
- What their preferred activity was
- Did they initiate communication for anything, and if so, how?
- Did they get excited about anything? How did they communicate that?
- Did they get frustrated about anything? How did they communicate that?
- How did you ensure they understood what you were telling them or asking of them?

4. Develop Interview Protocols for Consent and Dissent with EMLADs

Wherever possible, conduct interviews with your emergent bilinguals labeled as disabled (EMLADs), particularly bilingual nonspeaking students. Gathering data from your students' families and establishing a strong collaborative relationship with families is important, but the child is and should be the center of all that we do. Returning to the Communication Bill of Rights, we should talk to and with our students wherever possible, rather than talking about them.

Using a protocol for interviewing and collaborating with these children themselves is crucial. Snelgrove (2005) suggests a protocol for establishing consent in interviews with children with significant disabilities that presents opportunities for children to express agency during an interview process in ways that are easily understood by the interviewer/communication partner. In her article "Bad, Mad, Sad," Snelgrove traces her process, establishing shared cues for indicating consent or dissent to interview participation with disabled students. Snelgrove and the students reviewed signals that did not require spoken language, like putting one's head down or walking away, as forms of dissent when students did not wish to participate in an interview. Developing a protocol like this with the children you work with not only helps empower them to communicate their interest or disagreement, but also helps develop protocols around consent with children for whom decisions are often made without their input.

Be sure to incorporate translanguaging and opportunities for multimodal expression. If students in your class use communication devices, be sure to program them using the vocabulary words needed for the consent/dissent activity in all the languages they use. If you are using visual cards or boards, be sure to label the pictures with words in all the languages that students use. As in the Snelgrove example above, and like the example of my system with Kenny, you can also create hand signals or specific gestures that signify a student's interest or disinterest in participation—and be sure to provide explanations of these signals in all the languages your students use. These are just a few examples of how you can create space for translanguaging and multimodal expression.

5. Position and offer yourself as a co-conspirator, ally, and advocate with/for children and families.

Families of nonspeaking bilingual children are often at the intersection of several historically marginalized groups (Padía & Traxler, 2021). As such, families may feel disempowered within the educational system. Despite IFSPs and IEPs having legal safeguards protecting and upholding the rights of parents, guardians, and children themselves, many families still defer to educational and medical professionals. Some of this happens because they have been convinced that the educational professionals know what is best for their children, and sometimes it comes from a place of fear of schools and services as extensions of the federal government. This is particularly salient for undocumented or mixed citizenship status families. Sharing child and family rights explicitly with your students and their families, and sharing the ways that you can advocate and act according to the child and family's wishes, can ensure that all families are engaged in a way that leads to reciprocal carryover. If families are fearful of sharing their full selves and stories with us as educators, it can impede the pathway to true partnership and co-construction of learning.

6. Funds of Knowledge Evaluation

Taking a "funds of knowledge" (González et al., 2005) approach to students and families aligns with the notion of reciprocal carryover. Identifying community assets that may not be captured, represented, or acknowledged in educational curriculum or formal learning spaces can expand our capacity to help children grow. When we are able to tap into a wide range of knowledge—especially to uplift familial and community knowledge that we as educators may not already be aware of or well versed in—we signal to our students and their families that we are committed to learning together. This upends the notion of educational professionals as the experts and the children and families as non-knowers and places us in community to learn with and from each other and to grow accordingly.

Look at several different aspects of your students' communities and consider their funds of knowledge in each domain. Examples include but are not limited to (a) languages used, (b) values and traditions, (c) caregiving, (d) educational activities, (e) family outings or activities, (f) household chores and responsibilities, (g) favorite TV shows or singers, (h) family occupations or hobbies, and (i) scientific knowledge. Go through this list and identify at least one fund of knowledge in each domain. Then look at a lesson or unit and identify how and where you can weave that into your practice and communication with the student.

7. Communication Bill of Rights

Consistently visiting the Communication Bill of Rights (Brady et al., 2016) can help ensure that all practices in your classroom/session space align to support the full communicative rights of the young person. Using the Bill of Rights as a checklist can help us evaluate our own practice on a regular basis to ensure that we are engaged in humanizing communicative pedagogy.

8. TrUDL—Translanguaging Universal Design for Learning

Considering the intersections of multilingual and multimodal materials, directions, tasks, and opportunities for expression is key for our students who are both bilingual and nonspeaking (Cioè-Peña, 2021a). Examining our curriculum and practices through a lens of TrUDL can help us identify areas where we can incorporate more multilingualism and/or increase the multimodal resources and opportunities for expression in our learning spaces. Using this framework to examine all parent/caregiver communication also ensures a clear and open pathway to bidirectional sharing of information in the language(s) and mode(s) that feel best for the families of our students.

As we discussed in previous chapters, there is a long and problematic history of conflating nonspeaking with low intelligence. It is important that as educators we do not make the mistake of assuming that because a child does not communicate in normative spoken ways, they do not understand complex concepts or information. Keeping our expectations high for all our students is key, but we can only do that when we involve students as active agents in their own learning processes. Table 4.2 provides a protocol for

Table 4.2. Student-Facing Accommodations Protocols

Student-Facing Accommodations Protocol
1. Print/present the child with their accommodations. Be sure to prepare materials aligned with the student's varied communication modes, including but not limited to AAC devices, picture symbols, and communication boards. Where appropriate, introduce the child to the symbol or word related to their accommodation and do a lesson introducing the vocabulary word to help them connect the item or action of their accommodation (such as noise-canceling headphones, a cardboard wall divider, and materials on a computer instead of paper).
2. Have the symbols or word descriptions of the accommodation(s) on their desk and support them in identifying how to access the accommodations, and how those accommodations *should* be provided in every class/learning space. Note that this practice underscores the importance of accommodations, keeps them at the forefront of everyone's mind, and promotes visibility of accommodations as a norm rather than something to hide or be ashamed of.
3. Role-play them requesting/identifying their accommodation needs if/when they are *not* being provided or readily available to them.
4. Note: "Accommodations" is a big word that can be confusing. Be sure to explain it to the child as "supports or things that help you learn best or help you meet the learning objective(s)," but continue to use the word accommodations to support the student's familiarity and comfort level with the terminology of their IEP.

involving students in evaluating the accommodations that their IEP lists for them, and determining which are helpful for them. Involving students in this way also provides data for us to use as teachers to integrate into every annual rewriting of an IEP to ensure that the updates are based on what the student indicates works for them, not just on our adult interpretations and projections of what works for them (Padía, 2024). Table 4.3 provides a template to support students in self-reflection around which accommodations help them with their learning process and in what ways.

As mentioned in the opening of this section, all of these tools are presented in this chapter in English, but in order to use them effectively with your students and their families, you should ensure they are translated into the languages the students and families use. Some districts will provide IEPs automatically in the parent or guardian's preferred language, whereas others will provide translations given verbally by school staff while the written document remains in English. Because an IEP is a legal document, it should be provided in the language that families feel most comfortable with. If, however, the IEP is provided only in English, ask your school or district's special education coordinators what translation services are available to

Table 4.3. Accommodations KWL Self-Reflection Chart

K (My accommodations I know I can use)	W (How I want to use my accommodations today)	L (Reflection on the day/period's learning)
Accommodation(s): ___ ___ ___ ___	Tools I plan to use to help me meet my goals: ___ ___ ___	What helped me learn best today? ___ ___ ___

you. Having the official IEP document in all the languages the student and family use will help you with these activities—especially with being able to share with the student themself about the accommodations that they are entitled to. We are trained as educators to follow the systems that our schools use—whether those are language systems like bilingual education program structures or special education systems like IEP-mandated services. While this is an important and legal requirement of our job, it is not enough to ensure we are attending to our students' full selves. Using protocols like the ones described here can help us pair the official systems with the informal, expert communication systems that families and children create.

CHAPTER 5

Intent to Communicate and the Perceiving Subject

> There's really no such thing as the "voiceless." There are only the deliberately silenced, or the preferably unheard.
>
> —Arundhati Roy

EXPANDING WHAT "COUNTS" AS COMMUNICATION IN THE CLASSROOM

I was teaching kindergarten, 1st-, and 2nd-grade self-contained special education in the basement of a school my second year of teaching. The basement had been split into two "classrooms" using bookshelves as dividers. There was no sound barrier between the two sides of the room. Two of the corners on my half of the room were occupied with desks, one for the school's speech therapist and the other for two of the school's cluster teachers. The speech teacher would see kids in her corner for one-on-one sessions, and the cluster teachers would sit in their corner and talk and plan during their prep periods. I say all this to point out, at its baseline, it was a very chaotic classroom experience with a great deal of auditory and sensory input. When you added into the equation that both the classes in this basement room were considered to be the most restrictive settings of six students, one teacher, and one paraprofessional (6:1:1), and children were placed in these rooms because they were deemed to need small class settings with more intensive supports, the reality of this room was not meeting their IEP-outlined needs from the onset.

One student in my class, a minimally speaking bilingual 1st-grader who we will call Nathaniel, was very committed to his daily routines. The day my assistant principal came in to do my teacher observation, he got visibly upset and kept pointing at her repeatedly, then pointing to the door. His message to her was clear: "You do not belong here." Another week, Nathaniel's speech therapist was scheduled to be at a workshop on Tuesday, the day she usually saw Nathaniel for their sessions. On Monday, she came in to prepare him: "Ms. Becca will be gone tomorrow, so we will have speech on Thursday this week, *not* on Tuesday." He looked at her and nodded, so she left, assured that he understood the change in schedule. The next day, Tuesday, I made sure to set up Nathaniel's visual daily schedule without speech on it. When 10 A.M, his usual speech time rolled around, Nathaniel went and stood by his schedule and his eyes began to fill with tears. I reminded him that Ms. Becca was away and would be seeing him on Thursday. I took his speech schedule icon and showed him where I put it on our classroom calendar for Thursday, saying in both English and Spanish that speech would happen on Thursday instead of Tuesday that week for him because Ms. Becca had a workshop and was not at school on Tuesday. He shook his head and repeatedly tried to move his speech symbol to Tuesday on his own daily schedule. Finally, to ease his tears and insistence, I let him keep the icon on his Tuesday schedule, but I took a dry erase marker and crossed out the laminated image and above it wrote Jueves (Thursday). This calmed him and his tears slowly subsided. He seemed to understand that I acknowledged that speech was *supposed* to happen that day, but also reassured him that it would occur another day, despite it not happening when it was meant to. We could have easily changed the schedule without considering Nathaniel's feelings and shut down his communication when he was expressing his distress at the change. Part of our work as educators is to honor and respond to the communication of all of our students. When our nonspeaking bilingual students share their thoughts, feelings, and ideas with us, it is our job to remain as open as possible to all of the ways they express themselves beyond spoken words. For Nathaniel, this meant paying attention to his facial expressions, his tears, his body orientation, his gestures, and the way he moved and manipulated visuals and items in the classroom to indicate his feelings. It also meant using our spoken words in both Spanish and English to ensure that we were giving him all the information he needed and that we were comprehending his needs and wants as fully as possible.

KEY IDEA(S)

Shortly after I moved to Chicago, I met a father of two young autistic boys. Their family was originally from Durango, Mexico. I asked him if the boys, who were born in the United States, were bilingual. He replied, "They don't speak much, so if you tested them, they wouldn't test as fluent in either language. But they live bilingual lives." I have thought about this conversation almost daily since then. While it seems common sense that a bilingual person lives a bilingual life, there is such deep importance in this statement for children who are written off as noncommunicators because they don't speak. Nonspeaking children are often written out of our imagination of what it means to be bilingual and what it means to be biliterate. If we reconceptualize literacy to think about the ways we read meaning in the world, there are so many ways that nonspeaking bilingual children, even young ones who aren't yet reading written or printed text, are bilingual and bicultural. They respond to communication in multiple languages. They recognize characters from movies and shows in multiple languages. They hum and clap and dance along to songs in multiple languages. They respond to symbols and signs from products from multiple countries, with labels in multiple languages. They may not speak in either language, but they engage with both languages and multiple forms of expression on a daily basis. *They live bilingual lives.*

Within this framing, how we perceive nonspeaking bilingual children's communication plays a huge role. While standardized tests might not consider students "fluent" in either named language, do we, the adults in these children's lives, consider them fluent language users?

When I was a first-year teacher, I attended a series of workshops at the district for new teachers of students with autism. One phrase that the instructor drilled into us was "All behavior is communication." If all behavior is communication, then are we not inherently recognizing the intentionality of every child as autonomous communication, regardless of what format, language, or modality their communication takes? The problem is not with our framework around behavior as a form of communication, but around the ways that we, as perceptive partners, interpret and project our own understandings and assumptions onto the communicator's intention (Goldin-Meadow, 2015; Padía, 2023). A pedagogy of perception encourages us to reconsider how we perceive, police, and attempt to control behavior—and, subsequently, communication. When we consider school metrics like the English language proficiency exam I had to administer to my bilingual nonspeaking students (from the opening in Chapter 4), we see how this perception gets systematized. I had to check a box saying that my students did not attempt to answer the questions in the Speaking portion of the test. This response was recorded as part of their official state language record. How did I know they were not attempting to figure out the response in their heads? If they were given assistive technology, would they have attempted to respond using those tools? The way we ascribe meaning to our perceptions of student behavior has severe implications for their educational trajectories—particularly for our nonspeaking bilingual students.

In schools, Functional Behavioral Assessments (FBAs) and Behavioral Intervention Plans (BIPs) are used to analyze, track, and then attempt to "correct" behavior that is considered problematic, that is considered to be a barrier in the child's learning or the learning of the classroom and school community. Both are legally binding documents, often used in service of mandated supports via a student's IEP. The FBAs identify the problematic behavior and details pertaining to said behavior, and both the FBA and BIP ask educators to identify what the desired outcome of the behavior is. This desire is framed in terms of function—that is, what the student is attempting to gain or what they are attempting to avoid. We must rethink *function* in terms of desired item/action or avoidance toward intention and perceiving the range of humanity of a child—not just *function* but thoughts, emotions, and what they intend to convey in a holistic way beyond reductive language of *gains* and *avoidances*. What about the communication of emotion? If we view all behavior as communication, and also as performing a desired outcome, is the function then a desire to be perceived? What if we thought of behavior's function in this way—as a desire to be perceived, rather than to gain or avoid something? How might that support our humanization of our students and also strengthen our own perceptive skills? As we saw with my former student Nathaniel, behaviors that are often read as refusal to do schoolwork or to follow directions may actually be an expression of distress. I had to communicate with Nathaniel in both Spanish and English, as well as using a range of visuals and gestures, to perceive that he was upset about his speech therapist's changing schedule.

Additionally, the FBA and BIP are premised on constructs of "skill deficit" versus "performance deficit" that must be problematized. Skill deficit is defined as something the child cannot yet do, whereas performance deficit is defined as something the child knows how to do but performs inconsistently. Particularly when it comes to young children and children with disabilities, if there are issues with executive functioning and/or self-regulation, how do we accurately separate skill and performance? Further, to imply that a child is *able* to do something but is not doing it consistently assigns blame when the child does not exhibit that skill. It is important to note that I have never encountered an FBA that asked whether the child was receiving communication and opportunities for expression in all the languages they use.

When I went over the concept of FBAs and BIPs with my graduate students, all of whom are early childhood educators, I asked them to complete an FBA with a particular student in mind. Across the board, every single one of them identified the issue as "performance deficit." All my students were thoughtful, critically minded educators. The educators who employ these tools are not the problem; the constructs are the problem. We must understand that educators read and respond to behavior through the ideological lenses of the institutions that trained us. When individual educators engage in actions that harm or demean students, I do not believe it is because these teachers are each a bad or malicious actor. Rather, we must acknowledge and then shift the ways that competence, intelligence, and agency have been constructed by our medical-educational systems through psychological and communicative pathology.

THE STATUS QUO: PROBLEMATIC CURRENT PRACTICES

A bilingual speech language pathologist I interviewed talked about Niveyah, a 4-year-old nonspeaking bilingual child, as being "totally nonverbal" and claimed, "She has no intent to communicate." This quote is not indicative of an evil speech therapist, but of the ideologies that we are trained into and expected to teach within as professional educators. This chapter explores how we define and understand the intention behind children's communication. Schools and teachers impose notions of what signals "intent" and "intentionality" in communication. Schools often conflate "nonverbalism" with low intelligence because school professionals are not equipped to be good perceptive partners to nonspeaking bilingual children.

I wonder often about how narrowly we conceptualize bilingualism. I won a prominent Bilingual Education dissertation award for the study that prompted this book, and one of the things that the committee cited as important about the study was that they had never really thought about bilingual nonspeaking children before. When we define bilingualism, the privileging of orality is one of the greatest limitations in how we conceptualize languaging (Brea-Spahn & Bauler, 2023; Padía, 2023). María Rosa Brea-Spahn was one of the first people who got me really thinking about this dynamic when she identified ways of languaging that include the gestural, like the example shared in Chapter 1 of using your mouth or chin to point at something instead of your hands and fingers. This intersection of culture and embodied language is so salient for our bilingual nonspeaking youth, but also for all of us; understanding that pointing is not limited to one's hand but might include one's mouth or face requires us to be culturally curious and aware human beings who acknowledge diversity of not just spoken language but all modalities of communication.

María Cioè-Peña, a mentor-friend who paved the way for a lot of bilingual special education research and transformative teaching, shared that a mother in one of her studies described her nonspeaking child's bilingualism when she said, "Entiende pero no lo habla" ("He understands but he doesn't speak it") in reference to Spanish language (Cioè-Peña, 2021a). The child literally didn't speak, but he understood Spanish; while they may not use vocal language, the mother recognized that her child *used* the language. What if we said families who *use* Spanish and English, instead of families who *speak* Spanish and English? How could we be more inclusive of our students/children who are not speaking Spanish but are using it? In this conversation, it is imperative to move beyond the idea of "expressive" and "receptive" language. Traditional language theories tell us that there are two primary types of language use: expressive, wherein someone is communicating outwardly, expressing an idea or thought to another person beyond themself (which may take the form of speaking, writing, gesturing, etc.), and receptive, which indicates that a person is receiving a message from someone else and making meaning of the *intended* message. In schools, receptive language skills are typically measured through checks for understanding and comprehension assessments to see what information that was shared with a child (whether orally, in written form, via visuals, etc.) was comprehended and how that comprehension aligns with the intended original message. The problem with this binary of receptive and expressive communication is that it breaks our communication down into very black and white forms. For example, when we are the receivers of nonspoken communication, like Niveyah's, but we perceive it as lacking "intent to communicate," typically those adults who are speakers are viewed as successful receptive languaging beings, and so the child is the one who must be ineffectively expressively communicating. The question of the expressive intent and the receptive interpretation plays a huge role in who gets identified as an intentional communicating subject and who gets to make meaning.

What does this mean for our perceptive partnerships? How do we engage in community through our communication in a way that honors the intentionality of all communicators? Can we identify and recognize moments when we do not receive or perceive fully, and rather than blaming the expressing child for their lack of clarity, take ownership for our lack of perceptive skills to effectively comprehend their full message? Why does the person who speaks always get to determine whether or not there is comprehensible meaning in the exchange?

To answer these questions, we need to examine the norms and rules of power that govern our school systems. Building on Teaching in Action strategies from previous chapters, in this chapter we will extend our analyses of concepts like the culture of power and the Four I's of Power and Oppression to consider how we approach and understand our students' behaviors and intentions—and how we can continue to develop our perceptive skills to understand them even better.

LEARNINGS FROM CHILDREN, FAMILIES, AND EDUCATORS

Quirks as Intentions

Susana shared that Emmanual did not interact much with other kids when he was younger, preferring to play with Legos, blocks, or his hands, and also that he did not like to watch TV. She shared, "He would hide my things, like I would be looking for lipstick, for example, and it would be under his pillow. Like he would take things and hide them; it was the weirdest thing." Despite identifying this as *weird*, Susana clearly recognized that this behavior was communicating something, as she named the items he would hide his *obsessions.* Susana recognized Emmanual's intent to communicate his interest in an object or item when he engaged in the action of hiding it. Despite her sharing that the thing that helped her understand him the most was Emmanual "learning how to speak . . . and learning those [high-frequency] words," her anecdote about the systems they created with the routines, as well as her attention to his behaviors and what they indicated about his interests, shows that she perceived his communication as intentional, even when she did not fully understand his thought process or reasoning.

Emmanual and I discussed how he communicated with his teachers. He said that he let them know when he was feeling upset "by how I work . . . and how I talk," and shared that he lets them know when he's really into something when he "laugh[s] and get excited." Emmanual, as a child who was nonspeaking for most of his life and only began expressing himself with spoken language in the past 3 years, recognized that he still expressed himself to people primarily through unspoken actions and indicators. His recognition that he expressed himself through his work style and his laughter and emotiveness speaks to the fact that his teachers probably understood these nonverbal cues as intentional communication. This example highlights what many teachers already know and enact—that we communicate with students using so much more than just words. We must extend this understanding to our students who do not use spoken words and to recognize these forms of expression as *not just companions to spoken language, but forms of expression and communication in their own right.*

Whining as a Form of Intention: All Behavior Is Communication

Hector's Applied Behavior Analysis (ABA) provider Kayla talked about her process of getting Hector to communicate, but what she clearly meant was to communicate using spoken words. ABA is a form of therapy that is typically used with individuals with autism or other developmental disorders to increase "positive" behaviors and decrease "negative" ones. ABA is controversial because it presumes there are universal desirable and undesirable behaviors, and some people feel that the methods are so strict and repetitive that they are dehumanizing. Fiona, however, expressed a positive experience with ABA for her child. Kayla, the ABA therapist, said,

> The biggest thing was getting him to communicate, so if he's whining you're not responding to the whining, you are modeling, you know a sentence for him. What do you want? I want so and so. Or, I need this or I feel like this way, so again just really trying to model how to express himself.

While there is not necessarily anything wrong with working to help him express himself using spoken words, it is important to acknowledge that unspoken expression is valid and valuable communication. She identified him as whining and said that she was modeling how to express himself. Whining *is* a form of expressing himself. If what we mean is that we are working on expression with spoken words, we must be explicit about that. Reading whining as unintentional, uncommunicative behavior is just flat-out incorrect. As many behavior specialists like to say, *all behavior is communication* (Michigan Alliance for Families, 2024; Morin, 2024).

She clearly did this out of concern for him; in fact, she expressed the same concern as Fiona when it came to him being able to express himself in a way that others would understand. Kayla said:

> The BIGGEST thing is always for me language. Tell me what you want, expressing yourself, if you're feeling a certain way, tell me. Because there would be times when he would just cry, and I didn't know. He wanted his mommy. She would go to another room, and oh so I need mommy, I want mommy. And it's okay, but you know getting him to use those words, 'cause again, children go to school. I'm a teacher, tell me what you want, 'cause we can't always guess . . . And if anything happens to you, you're able to tell another person or another adult what happened.

This quote demonstrates Kayla's deep concern with the child being able to express himself in a way that will be perceived by others. This does not come from a place of ill intention; Kayla's attitude mirrors that of many educators. We want to support our students in getting what they need, in being able to be understood and being able to share their emotions, wants, and needs with others and to be heard and perceived. This is a perfect example of how we can more fully support our nonspeaking bilingual children—and all our children—by tuning into the ways they communicate without spoken words. Because not all of our children will develop spoken language tools to share their thoughts and feelings, we must learn to develop perceptive language tools to understand communication that comes in different forms. When a child is crying, or rocking, or flapping their arms, or making a certain facial expression, rather than placing the onus on them to use their words, can we place the onus on ourselves to use our perceptive tools? Kayla did later indicate that she pays attention to the nonverbal cues that children exhibit, but her use of the words "little kids" and "baby" seems to indicate the mindset that we must be attuned to nonverbal cues when children are in their infancy, before typical oral language development is expected. Once children hit the age where they are typically expected to begin speaking (American Speech–Language–Hearing Association, 2024), there seems to be a shift to considering communication in terms of vocal oral word use. Because of this, we can learn from early childhood educators, who are often clued into communication beyond spoken language. We must extend this understanding to older kids as well, because we don't stop using these nonverbal expressions once we start using spoken words, and for those children who do not start using spoken words, it is crucial that we consider a range of expression(s).

Kayla went on to say,

> I understood his body language. You know when you work with little kids, I become very attuned, in tune to my baby [the ABA client/child being serviced], so I'm always checking in. . . . I'm just quiet and I'm just looking at the baby, okay, let me see, something's going on. I try to be very proactive. So before they start the whining or before I notice they may not want something, you know I'm reading his facial cues, body language . . . And that's usually my cue to either end an activity or let's take a break or mommy you know maybe he wants a snack, so just again, he was very communicative. He wasn't a child where I didn't know what was the matter.

Despite her earlier note that he wasn't communicating when he was whining, here we see her recognizing that he was "very communicative." When we really stop and unpack our understandings of communication, most of us as educators do in fact recognize that kids communicate beyond just spoken language. Unfortunately, we privilege spoken language so much as kids get older that children who do not use spoken words are considered to be intentionless or, if they are bilingual, regarded as oxymorons who couldn't possibly exist. And yet, they very much do exist, and they very much do have intention, like all people.

Children Have Intentions Even When Adults Can't Access or Read Them

Bernardo's mom Florence described the differences in how they as his parents understood him at home versus how he was understood by people at school when she said,

> I mean at home we don't really have much trouble understanding him, we sort of know when he has his own way of saying something we understand what he's talking about, I mean we did get a note from the preschool once letting us know that he was just pointing and crying when he wanted something, and they were trying to focus on him using his words.

Here Florence identified that as his parents/family, they understood both his vocalizations and what he expressed nonverbally, but at school when he didn't use spoken words, the school staff did not recognize his communication as legitimate or legible. She did say that while they have told her that "they're trying to remind him to use his words instead of just crying and pointing when he wants something," the school staff "haven't officially raised any concerns with us" regarding his speech and language development. Again, this is likely because he was a young child; young children tend to receive more grace and understanding when they exhibit more non-vocal expression, as they are closer to the typical age when spoken language first starts to develop (Goldin-Meadow, 1999).

In Chapter 1, we learned about children *stimming*, what is often thought to be a shortened term for stimulating or self-stimulating. Stimming is often used to describe behaviors like rocking back and forth, spinning in a circle, or flapping one's hands. When I first started teaching, I was taught that these behaviors are inappropriate and that we should work to get rid of them with our students, replacing them with "more appropriate" behaviors instead. However, as I spent more time teaching, I began to learn that stimming is in fact an extremely useful self-soothing and self-regulatory practice that children employ to calm themselves down when they are overstimulated. I had a 1st-grade nonspeaking bilingual student who would hold a pencil in front of his face, right up near his line of vision, and shake the pencil. I was told by district autism trainers that year that this was called "perseverating," and it meant that my student was fixating on an object or motion in an inappropriate and unhealthy way. I was told that stimming and perseverating had no intention, that these were automatic physical reactions that many students with autism had that they could not control, so it was the teacher's job to help them control and extinguish these behaviors. I came to realize, however, that this was the child's way of comforting himself when he was overwhelmed with the amount of materials involved in an activity, the amount of noise occurring in the classroom, or the number of people present around him. When I asked him comprehension questions in Spanish and gave him visual card options to respond directly following his holding a pencil in front of his face, he always responded correctly. He was listening and engaging, and his stimming and "perseveration" was, like my student who looked away when he was concentrating on auditory input, actually helping him get himself in the right mindset to internalize information. Removing a child's stims from their options when they are overwhelmed is harmful to their learning process. Just as I learned with my Vietnamese student that the school's philosophy on eye contact was wrong, I learned that stopping students from stimming was also detrimental to their personal and academic growth. These physical movements, like waving a pencil in front of one's face or turning one's eyes to the floor during conversation, were full of intention and purpose for my students. They were not, as my professional development suggested, involuntary movements that we needed to help students unlearn. I was the one who needed to unlearn what I had been taught about these movements and relearn them as intentional, important, and valuable moves on the part of my students.

Educators' Language Ideologies With Nonspeaking Bilingual Children

Just as I myself held problematic language ideologies with my nonspeaking bilingual children, like the ones above regarding stimming and perseverating, many of us approach our nonspeaking bilingual children with deficit perspectives, because that is how we are trained by our fields to understand language and behavior. I asked Ofelia to talk about one of her 4-year-old nonspeaking bilingual clients. I asked, "How does Niveyah communicate?" Her answer reflected a lot of assumptions and presumptions about what it means to have an "internal voice" and intentionality—just like the ones I was taught when I began teaching.

> That's an interesting question because I don't think she is aware that she has a voice to communicate with. She's very . . . [long pause] she'll imitate everything. But none of it is independent, maybe it's like more cries, but I don't think she realizes that she has an actual internal voice to get her message across, or sometimes she might want something but she won't say it. Maybe sometimes she'll like go for gesture, but very little. . . .

Her response is fascinating because it was not just about what the child is expressing, but here we see an analysis regarding the internal dialogue that a child has with herself; here we see an assumption that because the child does not communicate in ways that the receiver understands/perceives as legitimate, the child must also not be able to perceive her own ideas, dialogue, and "voice." Just as I had to learn that my students who were stimming where engaging in self-regulation, and that students like Nathaniel who were crying were not merely overcome with uncontrollable emotion but were in fact using their full communicative toolbox to express themselves in a way they could be understood, it is a journey to relearn what "counts" as communication and what we can honor as intentional behavior from our students. Just because we as the educators do not know how to make sense of what a child is doing or how they are acting does not mean that the child has no sense of themself.

When I asked about Niveyah's interactions with her peers, Ofelia referenced the relationship with her sisters:

> . . . what I've noticed is that all she does is imitate them . . . but it's more of a Simon says kind of a thing . . . but not an actual engagement or interaction among a shared interaction, it's more just she just does whatever they say.

What makes this interaction "not a shared interaction"? Just because someone imitates another person does not mean that they are being controlled, nor does it mean they are not sharing an interaction together. Imitation is one of many forms of shared interaction. Not to infantilize Niveyah or others who imitate, but think for a moment about a baby who imitates clapping or certain head movements; we count that as a shared engagement, often even praising the baby for being so observant and intelligent as to be able to imitate an adult action. Why, then, as a child grows older, do we diminish the agency in that act of imitation and say that it has no agentic meaning, no independence, no awareness, no intention? We must rethink how we consider independence, interdependence, and agency within the context of imitation and communication (Yergeau, 2018).

When I asked Ofelia what had been most helpful in her work with Niveyah, she shared that modeling and at times hand-over-hand (guiding the child's hand with the adult's hand to complete a task, such as tracing or reaching for an item) was helpful. She also suggested that, "I think there's an underlying diagnosis that hasn't been, um, so because of that. . . ." It might be that educators' lack of familiarity with a range of disability diagnoses leads us to struggle with our nonspeaking bilingual students' communication. If we feel unprepared or ill equipped to support our students because we have not been trained to support them, that might influence our insistence that our students do not have a lot going on in terms of thought process and autonomy. If Niveyah *did* have an awareness and intentionality, that would require Ofelia, her SLP, to reckon with the fact that she wasn't effectively accessing that intentionality and agency within their sessions. For myself, when I realized that my students' stims like waving a pencil in front of their face or rocking back and forth were intentional, it forced me to confront my lack of perceptive skills and acknowledge that I had spent a good chunk of the year trying to get rid of behaviors that were helping my students learn. Identifying the lack in Niveyah was the easier choice and absolved Ofelia of the responsibility for her growth.

I don't say this to blame Ofelia; I say this to identify how the field positions children as problems in need of "fixing," and when they exist outside of what the field understands and knows how to "intervene" in, they get labeled as nonintentional—and oftentimes are spoken about in dehumanizing ways. This is very much in line with what some disability studies scholars refer to as a *medical model of disability*, which positions disability as a problem within the individual person that needs to be fixed, cured, or rendered more "normal" (Shakespeare, 2006). This is in contrast to a social model of disability, which suggests that individuals might have impairments but they only become disabled once the environment disables them; for example, a person using a wheelchair only becomes disabled once they need to gain entrance to a building that has stairs and does not have a ramp or elevator. In education, our system is premised on the notion that we must intervene and "fix" the "problems" with children who fall outside of "normal" classifications. This applies to both multilingual children and children labeled with disabilities, and particularly to our students who are both bilingual and nonspeaking. As we can see, this is a larger systemwide ideological approach, and not a problem that belongs to individual educators; I do *not* say this to vilify any individual educator or speech language pathologist. For many children, like Katrina, this particular SLP, Ofelia, was extremely effective in supporting their language and communication development. It might be that the field at large has a perceptive problem and needs to reconsider how we orient toward nonspeaking bilingual communication and linguistic expansion. When I asked what she believed would help Niveyah with her continued language development, Ofelia said:

> I highly recommend that she goes for a developmental pediatrician, for an evaluation, to be given more of the services, because once a week therapy for speech to me . . . is not enough. I feel like she needs other sensory-based supports, and a school-based or central-based facility.

Here Ofelia was explicitly naming that she did not feel that the speech services that she was able to provide to Niveyah were sufficient for her language development, but she also indicated that there might be more going on than she was currently diagnosed and identified for.

Ofelia went on to say that Niveyah would sit there for the whole session and not do anything; she was waiting for Ofelia to initiate.

> It's gotten to the point where essentially Niveyah can sit at the table for the entire 30 minutes, granted we don't do this but I'm pretty sure it could happen, without saying anything. She could just look at the wall and be perfectly fine without saying anything, but you know I'll sit there to see if she'll say anything like actually start engaging in the conversation, not even engaging just requesting, and I'll just fiddle with my hair, I'll type on my laptop if I'm writing notes, and she's imitating those behaviors.
>
> So now the echolalia has gone further, of not just vocal, it's more of physical. Um, there's no play, there's no true actual way of playing, everything is lining up . . . she knows colors and she'll just randomly label colors, or numbers.
>
> But she doesn't know what a number is realistically, doesn't know what an actual color would be if she would hear it, um, so yeah no play skills, no actual communicative intent. She knows you're there but doesn't know you're there.

To say that there is no play, to say that because Niveyah wasn't initiating contact with her during their 30-minute session when they're sitting at a table together, is a projection of one adult's understanding onto a child and her intentions. When she says she has "no actual communicative intent," that is the crux of the issue. To say "She knows you're there, but doesn't know you're there" also represents an analysis that is full of assumptions. Just as

I was taught that perseverating on an item was something bad and had no value, as educators we are taught that mimicking or echoing words and movements are undesirable forms of communication that have no value or intent. We are trained to believe that our professional understandings are the truth because they are made by individuals who have been educated in formal institutions and granted formal degrees that supposedly qualify us to make these assumptions with authority.

I wish I had asked what she meant by communicative intent, or how she knew that Niveyah didn't know she was there. This is also a journey for me—as an interviewer, as a researcher, as an educator—to learn to ask, "What do you mean by that? Help me understand," as my partner likes to say. What would it mean to take a curiosity stance, both toward ourselves as educators and toward our students? In reflecting on this moment of research, I believe I was not embodying a true pedagogy of perception, because I heard Ofelia's comments and it triggered something in me, and rather than trying to understand what she meant, I was intent on not uncloaking how offended I was. I focused on getting through the interview and the other questions, rather than actually probing and following up on the ideologies underlying her statements regarding Niveyah's agency, intentionality, and understanding (or lack thereof).

How many of us have sat in meetings about students and heard colleagues say something we found to be offensive about our students? When we sit in IEP meetings with other educators and hear extremely negative, deficit-oriented comments about what our students cannot do, we can use this curiosity stance to probe further. Asking, "What do you mean by that? Help me understand," and even asking, "What have you seen, heard, or experienced the student doing that makes you think that?" can help us get to a place of understanding. Probing additionally to ask what language(s) were being used and what modalities were employed when a certain behavior was observed can also help unearth what practices are occurring for and with our bilingual nonspeaking students. If the answers someone provides are different than what you have experienced with a student, you can then share those points of divergence and note on record that the child does not exhibit the same behaviors with different people or in different environments. Expanding our pedagogy of perception is not just about the way we attune to our students. It is also about the way we attune to our colleagues and everyone who impacts our students' learning experiences.

When I asked how Ofelia would describe or classify Niveyah, she replied:

> I would classify Niveyah as nonverbal. . . . Especially because she doesn't have that intent to communicate, doesn't have that intent to really [unintelligible] herself, and if I'm using that specific definition I think Niveyah may be the only one, only child that falls into that category. . . . Whereas if I'm saying nonverbal

> as opposed to no verbal output, not so much as like sign or gesturing, or actually that intent then I have, um, five who use alternate means.

Here we see a bilingual SLP draw a distinction between what is classified as "nonverbal" (Niveyah) versus "no verbal output" (other children she saw and serviced). She noted that what disgtinguished Niveyah as nonverbal was her lack of intention. She noted that some of the children she worked with had no verbal output, but since they had what she perceived as intention, she did not consider them nonverbal in the same way. The conflation of nonverbal identity with being intentionless is dangerous. It removes the responsibility of communication partners to perceive and places all responsibility on the speaker. We can read this interaction through a raciolinguistic perspective because the assertion that this Latina bilingual young disabled child had no intent to communicate because she did not communicate in ways that made sense to her bilingual SLP is rife with deficit viewpoints. As educators we must recognize that determining who has intention and who doesn't is filtered through our own personal perceptive lens.

Despite the deficit linguistic ideologies that our education field trains us into, most educators also learn how to self-reflect and identify our own shortcomings. Ofelia was no exception. In terms of not knowing how to best support Niveyah, or even identify the needs to begin to support, Ofelia got more candid about this as the interview progressed. When I asked how she would describe Niveyah overall, she really reflected on her own difficulty with describing her. Here, we saw her identifying a perceptive deficit in herself, though the training of SLP and professionalism is so strong that rather than say "I don't know how to perceive this child and how to support them," the knee-jerk response that's woven into the fabric of our professional understanding is "Because I don't know how to perceive this child and her communication, she must not have any intent to communicate."

> I will be honest, that is a little bit of a difficult question, actually this past semester I had an intern, and I was going over every patient, and I got to Niveyah, and they asked me like oh how would you describe her? And I was just like I I can't. . . . Because she's so . . . she doesn't fit in any category specifically. I would say this child has Down syndrome and they're showing their typical markers for Down syndrome you can use to track, but Niveyah is unique . . . like she has those red flags but also goes beyond that at the same time, and I mean there may be times when she'll surprise you with something, but in general she's like a very sweet little girl, um, she's adorable, when I think of her language overall or her as a student it's really hard to describe her because I feel like even after a year I'm still trying to figure that out, I'm still trying to learn, and you know really that kind of back-and-forth where you're speaking with a child, whereas

> it's a year now and I'm still at that figuring it out stage. So it's a big question. It's a big question that I don't know how to answer.

Recognizing when we do not have the answers, or even the analysis needed to support our students, is the first step in rewiring our perceptive partnerships with our students. We are also often taught to adhere to standardized milestones and metrics as educators and taught that only when our students meet those metrics are we successful educators. For someone like Ofelia, who speaks Spanish and is a trained bilingual therapist, it is worth noting that she did not leverage her own bilingualism much in Niveyah's sessions. Bilingual special educators are often referred to as "unicorns" and are in demand by school districts and agencies because of how rare they are—and how necessary they are for legal compliance for bilingual children with disabilities. Despite this, Ofelia did not seem encouraged to use her bilingualism as a strength and point of connection with Niveyah. This is another way that the system fails us as educators, and ultimately fails our students; we are discouraged from relying on our own lived experiences and expertise, and instead are taught to uphold normative standards of success.

I remember sitting where Ofelia was, feeling like I had only questions and no answers about how to support my bilingual nonspeaking students. The questions are the beginning. The questions are the key to rewiring how we view our students. In the questions we will find ways to recognize students' agency and communicative intent. When I asked questions about why Nathaniel would not stop crying or why he had planted himself in front of his daily schedule, I was able to start to identify that the words I had communicated to him were not sufficient for what he was requesting. He needed visual supports and assurance that his speech session was meant to happen that day, had been rescheduled, and would indeed happen on another day. His tears and standing still near his schedule were not involuntary—they were intentional.

When I asked what Ofelia's language goals were for Niveyah moving forward, she identified that she was working with her on initiating requests. Interestingly, she recognized that she had made advancements, which seems at odds with the notion that she has no communicative output or intentionality. She described her goals for her as follows:

> It's more just to kind of initiate . . . Like some form of communication, um, for her to . . . she's made gains, like such as she'll sit at the table now, she transitions, so those were really our main thing now . . . if she'll initiate a request . . . First. . . . if she will play functionally, um, and requesting I'll even go as far as, she'll tap me on the shoulder, or tap me on my arm and point to something, um, that's not even her goal at this point, everything is more of an intent to tell me that you want to play with something or that you want to play . . . Um, it's more

> of like those simpler, and you know, kind of seeing if she . . . I don't even wanna say like she'll produce some word approximations, she has words, so just more of, um, having the function to request.

Ofelia also talked about using PECS (Picture Exchange Communication System)—a system that uses printed picture symbols to teach children how to request various items using visuals—and gestural modeling with Niveyah. Again, we can see both things to be true here: Ofelia simultaneously understood the importance of expansive communicative tools and also believed that they should be leveraged in service of vocal communicative output, which she reified as the ultimate demonstration of intelligence, agency, and intentionality.

Ofelia talked a great deal about the importance of modeling communication. What I wonder with her is how she conceptualized this. She mentioned the use of multimodal strategies like gesture with Niveyah, and yet, when she explained Katrina's successful language development, the other child in the study who she supported, she described the importance of showing her "how we communicate." Here she referred to vocal communication, and the word choice reflects the ideology that spoken (English) language is the correct way to communicate. This entrenched ideology runs counter to a pedagogy of perception.

> I think Katrina really just needed some kind of support, 'cause it was like, ohh, it was just like a boom of language. It was just like, it, she exploded. Her language just she started thriving and I think she just kinda needed someone to give her that support and show her this is what, how we communicate, and also helping parents do that at home. . . .
>
> Ofelia acknowledged how different Niveyah was from the other children that she worked with:
>
> Um, no actually I've seen a lot children who came in, and granted I'm still treating them now for other things, something else, but I've had a lot of kids who I see who are initially nonverbal, and now are saying full sentences, and are working on their speech production and things like that.
>
> So, um, I actually, Niveyah is, that's why I say Niveyah is more of a complicated case for me, because she's so different than the rest.
>
> Um, but I am still learning, so it's more of a Katrina situation that I come across versus a Niveyah.

"Katrina situations"—meaning bilingual children who may begin with limited vocal speech but develop spoken words very quickly—are what most educators see and experience, as opposed to "Niveyah" situations—meaning children who are considered bilingual and nonspeaking or "nonverbal." When I left the classroom, I went back to graduate school precisely because I received training to support "Katrina" students, to encourage their continued oral language development. I received some training to support nonspeaking monolingual students, but I did not receive any guidance or support on best practices to understand and support "Niveyah" students. Katrina was identified in the interviews by both her parents and her SLP as being "eager to learn." This again points us to a pedagogy of perception: How are we identifying, measuring, and evaluating eagerness, enthusiasm, intention? Because Katrina responded in the spoken ways that not just her speech therapist, but society at large, desired her to respond in, she was identified as being an enthusiastic, eager participant.

> Uh, overall she what's the plant that kind of takes slow to grow? . . . she's like a little seed initially, and then when she left she like turned into a giant tree, with all the gains that she made. She was so receptive . . . to everything that we were doing, she was so participatory, she was really excited, and you could, she was eager to learn. I think Katrina was really, she was really eager to learn and take in all this language, and the best part of her was because of all that language, she just threw it out spontaneously. So she observed the language, and then just blurted it out to you.

Because Niveyah did not respond in the spoken ways that her speech therapist and society at large desired, she was identified as having no awareness or intention. As educators, we often celebrate the milestones that align with typical development. We are evaluated on how well we move our students toward these standardized milestones. Our principals and our schools are regarded highly when we move students toward general education standards for their assigned grade level. We are taught to celebrate students like Katrina. We are not taught to recognize and celebrate the communicative intent and growth in students like Niveyah. In Chapter 4, we saw how Niveyah and her sisters co-constructed their own system of communication. Niveyah's mother created systems of color identification and played guessing games with her to figure out what she wanted. Her family recognized and affirmed her intention to communicate and acknowledged her as a communication partner within their family. As educators, we have so much relearning to do to support, perceive, and celebrate "Niveyah students"—that is, our bilingual nonspeaking students.

COMMUNICATIVE JUSTICE TAKEAWAYS

In this chapter, we have explored the value of expansive communication and of reconceptualizing how we view intention. Nonspoken communication is just as valuable as spoken communication; the issue is that it is not *valued* in schools and society as much as spoken language. Expanding our conception of communication helps us become better teachers and communication partners and allows us to realize that nonspeaking bilingual children are bilingual people who live bilingual lives.

A child's spoken expression is not an indication of their internal process or their intent(ion). Employing the pedagogy of perception that we explored in Chapter 3 can help us hone our perceptive skills to learn from our students through the range of ways they express themselves. Both Kayla and Ofelia identified ways that children communicated with them in nonverbal modes, but the focus on spoken language is so entrenched in us as educational professionals that we can simultaneously acknowledge nonspoken overtures and blow right past them in our pursuit of information and intention through spoken language. Rewiring what we look, listen, and scan for as teachers can help us reconsider our students as agents with thoughts, feelings, and intentions that we can and should attend to and learn from. It is not only nonspeaking students who use a range of multimodal forms of expression. All of our students, even those who use spoken language, use expression like body language, gesture, facial expression, and nonspoken vocalizations (e.g., laughing, crying, screaming) to express their thoughts and feelings. In the next section, we will consider how to rewire our understandings of classroom communication and community to incorporate and honor these myriad forms of language and expression of ideas and intentions.

TEACHING IN ACTION

In this section, I present some resources to help us rethink what counts as intentional communication with our students. The Teaching in Action tools include suggestions for reimaging the ABC chart as a Conditions-Expression-Response (CER) checklist that honors multiple forms of expression, rather than simply identifying "problem behaviors" like the ABC chart does. We then explore a Pedagogical Integrity tool designed to help educators reflect on our own biases and ideologies about language. Unearthing what beliefs we have been taught and trained to believe about our nonspeaking bilingual children is the first step in working toward communicative justice and belonging for all students in our classrooms. Finally, we end with a Communication Bill of Rights Evaluation, a tool that helps us explore which communication rights are being affirmed, which are being denied, and how we as educators can adjust our classroom learning spaces to ensure that our students have all of their communication rights met.

Rethinking the ABC Chart

Earlier in the chapter, Fiona mentioned the use of an ABC (Antecedent-Behavior-Consequence) chart to help identify what was occurring with her son. The ABC chart is often identified as a tool to ascertain what in the environment is setting a child off, and what responses might be either exacerbating or supporting the "problem behavior." While ABC charts like the example shown in Table 5.1 can be useful in identifying conditions in the environment that are causing a child to react, the issue with the ABC chart is that it is meant to be used when a behavior that is considered problematic or challenging is occurring. In Table 5.2 I present an alternative to the ABC chart that I call the CER chart: Conditions-Expression-Response. This is a nonexhaustive checklist meant to help us as educators turn the lens on ourselves and on our communicative communities in our classrooms to determine what forms of expression we are missing or responding to in a negative way in the context of our classroom communities. The CER chart is a tool to help deepen our pedagogies of perception and increase our awareness of the types of expressions our nonspeaking bilingual children use that we may be missing in our daily practice. The Conditions section refers to the conditions in the learning environment at the time of observation. Expression relates to the focal student with whom the observation is being done. The Response category applies to all other people in the room, including you, as the primary educator, any co-teachers or classroom support staff, and other children in the classroom. The tool is meant to capture low-inference notes, meaning you do not include your own analysis in the checklist, but as much as possible write down exactly what you observe. Of course, all our observations are filtered through our personal interpretations, but capturing exactly what you see can be helpful; rather than saying, "Billy was crying because his toy got taken away," you can say, "Mr. E. picked up the toy that was on Billy's desk and walked to the other side of the classroom. Billy had tears coming out of his eyes and his nose was running; he was breathing heavily." The notes section below each checklist is where you can offer your own analyses and wonderings about what you observed, as well as set next steps for yourself and the classroom community based on what you noticed.

Pedagogical Integrity: Communicative Belonging

I present a model for Expansive Communication with Pedagogical Integrity (see Figure 5.1) with expansive communication in the classroom. It begins with convictions around all expression and communication being valuable and having a place of belonging in the classroom—what Souto-Manning and colleagues (2022) call "communicative belonging." This Venn diagram is a

Table 5.1. ABC Checklist Example

ABC Checklist

Student Name: ________________ Class: ________________

School:______________

Behavior of Concern: ________________________________

Date:	Time:	Location/ Setting:
Antecedent (before behavior)	**Behavior**	**Consequences (after behavior)**
Given direction/task/ activity	Refusing to follow directions	Verbal redirection
Asked to wait	Making verbal threats	Physical assist/prompt
New task/activity	Disrupting class (describe)	Ignored problem behavior
Difficult task/activity	Crying/whining	Kept demand on
Preferred activity interrupted	Screaming/yelling	Used proximity control
Activity/item denied (told "no")	Scratching	Verbal reprimand
Loud, noisy environment	Biting	Removed from activity/ location
Given assistance/ correction	Spitting	Given another task/ activity
Transition between locations/activities	Kicking	Interrupted/blocked and redirected
Attention given to others	Flopping	Left alone
Presence of specific person	Running away/bolting	Isolated within class
Attention not given when wanted	Destroying property	Loss of privilege
Left alone (no individual attention)	Flipping furniture	Calming/soothing:
Left alone (no appropriate activity)	Hitting self	verbal/physical/both
Other: ____________	Hitting others	Peer remarks/laughter
	Verbal refusal	Time-out (duration)__________
	Other: ____________	Other: ____________
Duration:	Intensity: ___ Low ___ Medium ___ High	Observer: ____________ Notes:

ABC Checklist adapted from theautismhelper.com

Table 5.2. Conditions-Expression-Response (CER) Checklist

Student Name:

Class:

Date:	Time:	Location/Setting:
Conditions (in learning environment)	**Expression (from student)**	**Response from educator(s), from peer(s), from other(s) after/during student expression**
• Lights on (specify type of light, such as fluorescent, LED) ______ • Lights off • Natural light in room (specify direct, indirect, and student's proximity to light) ______	• Body orientation (how does the student position their body? Who/what are they facing toward and who/what are they turned away from?) ______	• Body orientation (someone turned toward the student, turned away, etc. Name who and what body orientation changed in response to the student's expression) ______
• Ambient noise in room (list all) ______	• Eye gaze (where is the student directing their gaze?) ______	• Eye gaze (where is the student directing their gaze?) ______
• Assistive technology available (specify what AT is available and where it is in proximity to the student. Is the student aware of and able to access the AT independently?) ______	• Nonspoken vocal expression (what sounds is the student making? What words are they using? Could include laughing, crying, screaming, or others. You can either audio record and attach the recording or describe the vocalizations phonetically.) ______	• Nonspoken vocal expression (what sounds [that are not words] do others use in response to the student? Could include laughing, crying, screaming, or others and who gave the response) ______

• Assistive tech used (identify what AT is used by student) ______	• Gesturing (what gestures is the student making? This can include but is not limited to pointing, shrugging, hugging, touching, or reaching for a person or object, waving hands or arms, nodding or shaking their head, etc.) ______	• Gesturing (what gestures do others make in response to the student's expression? Identify who makes which gesture[s]) • Body movement (such as rocking, spinning, knocking their fist or head on furniture, clapping hands, etc.) ______
• People present ______	• Body movement (such as rocking, spinning, knocking their fist or head on furniture, clapping hands, etc.) ______	AAC use (what communication devices are used in response to the student and by whom? What is said with the device[s] and in what language[s]?) ______
• Proximity between student and others (specify distance and to whom) ______		
• Visual materials • Demand/directions placed on student (specify what demand[s]) ______	• AAC use (what communication devices is the student using and what is the output? What language[s] is it in? Are the options the students selected written words, drawn images, photographs, or some combination?) ______	• Facial expression (what facial expression do others have in response to the student? Are they smiling, grimacing, squinting their eyes, winking, etc.? Name who presents which facial expression[s]) ______

(*continued*)

Table 5.2. (*continued*)

Conditions (in learning environment)	Expression (from student)	Response from educator(s), from peer(s), from other(s) after/during student expression
• Direct auditory input (e.g., audiobook, audio played on smartboard, teacher speaking, peers speaking, etc.) ____	• Facial expression (what facial expression do you perceive on the student? Are they smiling, grimacing, squinting their eyes, winking, etc.?) ____ • Audience (who appears to be the intended audience of the student's expression? What makes you think this?) ____	• Spoken response (name what was said and by whom) ____ • Student provided with a familiar item (name who provided the item and what it is) ____ • Audience (are the responses to the student directed at the student or at other peers or teachers? How do you know?) ____
Notes: Questions: Next Steps:	Notes: Questions: Next Steps:	Notes: Questions: Next Steps:

Figure 5.1. Pedagogical Integrity: Expansive Communication in the Classroom

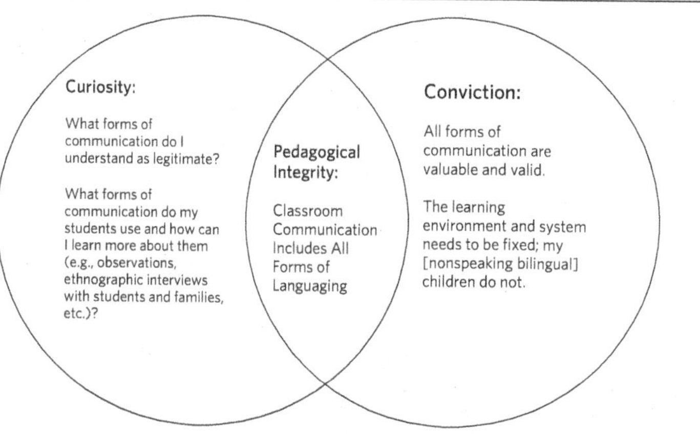

Adapted from Padía (2024).

tool for teachers to self-reflect on our own biases around language to begin to transform our classrooms into spaces of communicative justice.

Classroom Communication Rights

Finally, Table 5.3 presents a Communication Bill of Rights Evaluation using the American Speech–Language–Hearing Association (ASHA)'s Communication Bill of Rights to assess what rights are being upheld and which might be violated in your own classroom or learning community.

As we discussed in this chapter, much of the work of perceiving our bilingual nonspeaking students and their intentions begins with self-reflection and examining our own ideologies around language and communication. This chapter's Teaching in Action resources offer a mix of tools to reflect on our beliefs and practices as educators and tools to better understand our nonspeaking bilingual students and their experiences and expression within our classroom learning communities.

Table 5.3. Communication Bill of Rights Evaluation

Student Name:

Educator/Evaluator Name:

Date(s):

Right	Affirmative Example(s) **How is this right affirmed in the classroom for this child? Be as specific as possible.**	Misexample(s) **How is this right denied in the classroom for this child? Be as specific as possible.**	Next Steps/Action Items **How will you adjust your classroom (physical space, pedagogical strategies, multilingual resources/materials, multimodal resources/materials, etc.) to ensure the child has their rights met?**
1. The right to interact socially, maintain social closeness, and build relationships			
2. The right to request desired objects, actions, events, and people			
3. The right to refuse or reject undesired objects, actions, events, or choices			
4. The right to express personal preferences and feelings			
5. The right to make choices from meaningful alternatives			

6. The right to make comments and share opinions			
7. The right to ask for and give information, including information about changes in routine and environment			
8. The right to be informed about people and events in one's life			
9. The right to access interventions and supports that improve communication			
10. The right to have communication acts acknowledged and responded to even when the desired outcome cannot be realized			
11. The right to have access to functioning AAC (alternative and augmentative communication) and other AT (assistive technology) services and devices at all times			

(continued)

Table 5.3. (*continued*)

Right	Affirmative Example(s) **How is this right affirmed in the classroom for this child? Be as specific as possible.**	Misexample(s) **How is this right denied in the classroom for this child? Be as specific as possible.**	**Next Steps/Action Items** **How will you adjust your classroom (physical space, pedagogical strategies, multilingual resources/materials, multimodal resources/materials, etc.) to ensure the child has their rights met?**
12. The right to access environmental contexts, interactions, and opportunities that promote participation as full communication partners with other people, including peers			
13. The right to be treated with dignity and addressed with respect and courtesy			
14. The right to be addressed directly and not be spoken for or talked about in the third person while present			
15. The right to have clear, meaningful, and culturally and linguistically appropriate communications			

Adapted from ASHA Communication Bill of Rights.

Conclusion

Toward the end of the time that I was writing this book, I attended a session by Khawla Badwan at the British Educational Research Association (BERA) and World Education Research Association (WERA) in Manchester, UK. The presentation was on co-researching with children, and the children and other school staff members were co-presenting the session with Dr. Badwan. One of the themes presented in this session was the notion of hospicing education—that is, caring for a system that is in decline (de Oliveira Andreotti et al., 2015; Badwan et al., 2024). Within the notion of hospicing education is the dual existence of reimagining and rebuilding from what Badwan calls the "pockets of joy" that exist within this declining system. I offer this conceptual frame for communication: *What if educators think of ourselves as care workers hospicing normative communication in our schools?* Under this frame, we are not aiming to eradicate spoken, normative forms of languaging, but to sunset the cultural and social norms and structures of power that uphold white mainstream spoken English (WMSE) as the superior, dominant, primary, and/or expected form of communication in our learning spaces.

As we saw with children like Kenny, for some children and teachers this might look like the use of hand signals, drawings, and bilingual written notes as the primary form of expression. As we saw with children like Bernardo, for some this might mean use of multiple spoken languages used in small bursts to convey their point, like when Bernardo said, "I love it patos!" to share that he wanted to remove his shoes (zapatos). As we saw with the principal I met who had used her own money to install giant visual communication boards on the school playground, for some learning spaces this may mean teaching all students and staff how to use bilingual communication boards and devices so that it is not just the nonspeaking bilingual children who are expected to use devices to be perceived by the English speaking world, but speakers of English also learn to use communication tools beyond monolingual oral speech. Tiffany Hammond published a children's book (2023) called *A Day with No Words* where the mother, who does speak to communicate, will commit to entire days using a communication device as her nonspeaking son does so that she can experience what communication is like for him. Practicing multiple forms of expression and decentering WMSE as the goal in our learning spaces can help everyone—teachers and students alike—to understand the vast options for expression at our fingertips that span modalities and named languages, from facial expressions to gestures to body orientation to eye gaze to visuals to handwriting to typing and more.

At this same conference, Kris Gutiérrez delivered a keynote speech titled "Worldmaking for Just Educational Futures: A Utopian Vision and Methodology" (2024). An audience member asked her about the relationship between third spaces and utopian projects in education, and she replied that third spaces are utopian projects. Communicative justice currently exists as a third space, as a utopian project in education. It offers us the tools to dream, act, and communicate with one another beyond the confines of our current systems. Alexander Chee referenced Hannah Arendt by suggesting that freedom might mean the freedom to imagine that which we cannot yet imagine (2018). Learning from our bilingual nonspeaking students and their families can guide us toward that which we as educators cannot yet imagine, toward third spaces, toward utopian projects, and, ultimately, toward freedom. Families like Susana and Emmanual's who are counseled away from bilingualism help us imagine what a more just world might look like when it comes to communication for and with bilingual nonspeaking children. Despite the family being told not to use Spanish with Emmanual because of his disability, and despite the family following this advice, Emmanuel still picked up on and comprehended a great deal of Spanish, because he lived in a bilingual family. Though he did not speak Spanish, he lived a bilingual life. Our school systems must find ways to honor these lived realities of bilingual nonspeaking children as we dream and teach toward freedom. Infusing our classroom spaces, lessons, and opportunities for expression and engagement with multilingual, multimodal prompts, activities, and resources may seem like a small change, but it creates large ripples. It destabilizes WMSE as the norm and resets multilingual, multimodal communication as the common practice in our learning communities. Strategies like having multilingual books in the class library; sharing instructions in all the languages your students use including visual representations of instructions and tasks; and working with the speech teacher to ensure that a student's communication device or board is programmed in all the languages they speak are all ways to destabilize WMSE and engage in freedom dreaming toward communicative justice. Like my student who used his tablet to type out "veinti-six" as his answer to a math problem, when we provide our nonspeaking bilingual students with the space, support, and understanding to use their full linguistic repertoires, we will begin to perceive their brilliance and their whole selves.

Recently, someone told my colleague (an elementary classroom bilingual special educator teacher) and me that it must feel great that so few people are doing the type of research we're doing, so there's such a great need for our work. We looked at each other, sharing an unspoken understanding that no, it does not feel great. Nonspeaking bilingual children exist, even if the research doesn't. Teachers of nonspeaking bilingual children exist, even if the curriculum and teacher professional development doesn't. Just because the professional resources don't exist yet or aren't widely available does not mean that we can give up on supporting our nonspeaking bilingual children. I hope that the stories, suggestions, and resources in this book help you work collaboratively with your students, their families, and your colleagues to really commit to and enact communicative justice in your own learning spheres. While we have centered nonspeaking bilingual children, expansive communication benefits all learners. When we work on acknowledging *More Than Words*, like the children's book and activity in the Introduction suggests, we begin to nurture deeply empathetic, perceptive classroom communities where children and adults alike attune to communication that includes facial expressions, physical movements—including stimming, body placement and orientation, eye gaze, expressions of emotion like laughter and tears, gestures, visual cues, and various spoken named languages.

We have traveled together through various ideas and strategies for communicating and teaching beyond spoken words in this book. Specifically, I have shared how some of my own perceptive failures and missteps early on in my teaching career led me to develop new approaches to communicative justice, like a pedagogy of perception and communication communities. We met Veronica in Chapter 1, a student who used her perceptive skills to communicate to me how unhappy she was when I refused to let her erase her writing all morning like she wished. We examined her behavior as expression to the best of her ability and considered how my own perceptive failures led to this physical communication. We met Nasir in Chapter 2, a student who followed his love of coffee, which was appreciated at school, into a dangerous situation out in public. In school, we thought we were affirming his love of coffee and appreciating his endearing hunt for it, when in reality we were not teaching him the social boundaries necessary to keep him safe in a society that did not perceive him as the sweet child that he was, but as a threatening man. In Chapter 3, we learned about school language intake questionnaires, the process for identifying students as English learners, and the inadequacy of state English language proficiency tests to account for the expression of our nonspeaking bilingual children. In Chapter 4, we met Kenny, a bilingual minimally speaking student who spent weeks diving under desks for hours, until we figured out a system and process that worked for him to express himself using a combination of hand signals, drawing, and bilingual writing. Finally, in Chapter 5 we met Nathaniel, a student whose difficulty deviating from routine forced me to examine what expression I was silencing and ignoring as a teacher and how I could be a more receptive, responsive communication partner in the classroom.

In addition to the reflections from my time as a classroom teacher and instructional coach, we have learned from the experiences of the nonspeaking bilingual children, their families, and their educators who participated in the research study with me. The knowledge, expertise, and experience that families and children share is so rich and valuable, yet we have seen how rare it is that these families shared their wisdom with their child's educators. The onus is not on families to share this information; it is on us as educators to ask families about their knowledge and expertise, and to help them understand that we are on the same team. Families, especially those of bilingual nonspeaking children, so often hear school professionals tell them what their child cannot do and what is wrong with their child. Using tools like ethnographic interviewing and shared video reflections can help us communicate to families how serious and intentional we are about understanding, valuing, and nurturing every aspect of the nonspeaking bilingual child. It is not enough to just have multilingual resources like word walls in multiple languages or multilingual classroom libraries. It is not enough to just have monolingual multimodal resources like AAC devices, audiobooks for children to listen to, interactive white boards, and visual symbols. All of these components are important for rich classroom environments, but in order to enact communicative justice, we must consider how all of our lessons, activities, and interactions honor the intersections of multilingualism and multimodality. Our nonspeaking bilingual children do not live fragmented lives; they are whole people who exist at the intersections of racialization, multilingualism, and disability. They deserve holistic classroom spaces, perceptive pedagogies, and communication communities that honor their full selves. As you move toward communicative justice in your classrooms and learning environments, I hope the transformation illuminates the following truth: We *all* deserve holistic classroom spaces, perceptive pedagogies, and communication communities that honor our full selves. None of us is free until all of us are free. Developing our perceptive skills and expanding our communicative repertoires benefits all teachers and learners, as it unlocks new ways of interacting with and understanding one another and the world around us. We get free together.

References

Alim, H. S., & Paris, D. (2017). What is culturally sustaining pedagogy and why does it matter? In D. Paris & H. S. Alim (Eds.), *Culturally sustaining pedagogies: Teaching and learning for justice in a changing world* (pp. 1–21). Teachers College Press.

Alsace, T. & Colón, G. (2022). Preface. In G. Colón & T. Alsace (Eds.), *Bilingual special education for the 21st century: A new interface* (pp. xviii–xxxix). IGI Global.

American Speech–Language–Hearing Association. (2020). *Demographic profile of ASHA members providing bilingual services, year-end 2019*. www.asha.org

American Speech–Language–Hearing Association. (2024). *Communication milestones: Age ranges*. ASHA. https://www.asha.org/public/developmental-milestones/communication-milestones/

Annamma, S., Connor, D., & Ferri, B. (2013). Dis/ability critical race studies (DisCrit): Theorizing at the intersections of race and dis/ability. *Race Ethnicity and Education*, *16*(1), 1–31.

Artiles, A. J., & Ortiz, A. A. (2002). English language learners with special education needs: Identification, assessment, and instruction. Professional Practice Series, Center for Applied Linguistics. Delta Systems Co., Inc.

@backendzyy. (2024, January 6). *How yall feel bout this?* [Post]. X [formerly Twitter]. https://x.com/backendzyy/status/1743791713506730345

Badwan, K., Ratcliffe, T., & Seymour Park Community Primary School Children. (2024, September). *Research for collective thriving in education: A case of co-producing environmental research with children and teaching professionals in a primary school*. British Educational Research Association (BERA) Annual Conference. Manchester, UK.

Baker, C., & Wright, W. E. (2017). *Foundations of bilingual education and bilingualism* (6th ed). Multilingual Matters.

Baker-Bell, A. (2020). *Linguistic justice: Black language, literacy, identity, and pedagogy*. Routledge.

Blommaert, J., García, O., Kress, G., Larsen-Freeman, D., Adami, E., & Sherris, A. (2018). Communicating beyond diversity: A bricolage of ideas. In A. Sherris & E. Adami (Eds.), *Making signs, translanguaging ethnographies: Exploring urban, rural and educational spaces* (pp. 9–35). Multilingual Matters.

Boveda, M., & Annamma, S. A. (2023). Beyond making a statement: An intersectional framing of the power and possibilities of positioning. *Educational Researcher*, *52*(5), 306–314.

Brady, N. C., Bruce, S., Goldman, A., Erickson, K., Mineo, B., Ogletree, B. T., Paul, D., Romski, M. A., Sevcik, R., Siegel, E., Schoonover, J., Snell, M., Sylvester, L., & Wilkinson, K. (2016). Communication services and supports for individuals with severe disabilities: Guidance for assessment and intervention. *American Journal on Intellectual and Developmental Disabilities*, *121*(2), 121–138.

Brea-Spahn, M. R., & Bilingual Language and Literacy Investigative and Networking Group (BLLNG). (2023). *Mapping our languaging journeys and legacies: In community*. New York University. https://www.blling-slp.com/blog/http/www.blling-slp.com/blog-5

Brea-Spahn, M. R., & Bauler, C. V. (2023). Where do you anchor your beliefs? An invitation to interrogate dominant ideologies of language and languaging in speech-language pathology. *Language, Speech, and Hearing Services in Schools*, *54*(3), 675–687. https://doi.org/10.1044/2023_LSHSS-22-00135

CAST. (2024). *About Universal Design for Learning*. https://www.cast.org/what-we-do/universal-design-for-learning/

Chee, A. (2018). *How to write an autobiographical novel*. Bloomsbury Publishing.

Cioè-Peña, M. (2017). Bilingualism, disability and what it means to be normal. *Journal of Bilingual Education Research & Instruction*, *19*(1), 138–160.

Cioè-Peña, M. (2021a). "Entiende Pero No Lo Habla": Mother's definition of bilingualism for their children with disabilities. American Association of Applied Linguistics (AAAL). Virtual Conference. March 20–23, 2021.

Cioè-Peña, M. (2021b). TrUDL, a path to full inclusion: The intersectional possibilities of translanguaging and Universal Design for Learning. *TESOL Quarterly*, *56*(2), 799–812. https://doi.org/10.1002/tesq.3074

City University of New York–New York State Initiative on Emergent Bilinguals. (2017). *Teaching bilinguals (even if you're not one): A CUNY-NYSIEB Webseries*. CUNY-NYSIEB. https://www.cuny-nysieb.org/teaching-bilinguals-webseries/

@_colenewberry. (2018, January 17). *So do most children of immigrants but I guess it's less impressive when they're poor* @colenewberry [Reply].

Crais, E., Douglas, D. D., & Campbell, C. C. (2004). The intersection of the development of gestures and intentionality. *Journal of Speech, Language, and Hearing Research*, *47*, 678–694.

Crompton, C. J., Hallett, S., Ropar, D., Flynn, E., & Fletcher-Watson, S. (2020). 'I never realised everybody felt as happy as I do when I am around autistic people': A thematic analysis of autistic adults' relationships with autistic and neurotypical friends and family. *Autism*, *24*(6), 1438–1448.

Cummins, J. (1984). *Bilingualism and special education: Issues in assessment and pedagogy*. Multilingual Matters.

Cummins, J. (2008). BICS and CALP: Empirical and theoretical status of the distinction. In B. Street & N. H. Hornberger (Eds.), *Encyclopedia of language and education: Volume 2: Literacy* (2nd ed., pp. 71–83). Springer Science+Business Media LLC.

Daily Mirror [@DailyMirror]. (2018, January 17). *Princess Charlotte already speaks two languages at just two years old* [Post]. X [formerly Twitter]. https://x.com/dailymirror/status/953538632144564224

Danesi, M. (2022). *Understanding nonverbal communication: A semiotic guide*. Bloomsbury.

de Oliveira Andreotti, V., Stein, S., Ahenakew, C., & Hunt, D. (2015). Mapping interpretations of decolonization in the context of higher education. *Decolonization: Indigeneity, Education & Society*, *4*(1), 21–40.

Delpit, L. (1995). *Other people's children: Cultural conflict in the classroom*. New Press.

Ehlers-Zavala, F. P. (2011). Chapter 14: History of bilingual special education. In Rotatori, A. F., Obiakor, F. E., & Bakken, J. P. (Eds.), *History of special education* (pp. 343–361). Emerald Group Publishing Limited.

Emerson, R. M., Fretz, R. I., & Shaw, L. L. (2011). *Writing ethnographic fieldnotes*. University of Chicago Press.

Evans-Winters, V. (2023, April). *Intersectionality in teacher education. Division K Vice Presidential Session*. American Educational Research Association.

Flores, N., & García, E. S. (2020). Power, language, and bilingual learners. In N. S. Nasir, C. D. Lee, R. Pea, M. McKinney de Royston (Eds.), *Handbook of the cultural foundations of learning* (pp. 178–192). Routledge.

Flores, N., & Rosa, J. (2015). Undoing appropriateness: Raciolinguistic ideologies and language diversity in education. *Harvard Educational Review, 85*(2), 149–171.

García, O. (2019). Translanguaging: A coda to the code? *Classroom Discourse*, *10*(3-4), 369–373.

García, O., Flores, N., Seltzer, K., Wei, L., Otheguy, R., & Rosa, J. (2021). Rejecting abyssal thinking in the language and education of racialized bilinguals: A manifesto. *Critical Inquiry in Language Studies*, *18*(3), 203–228.

García, O., & Otheguy, R. (2020). Plurilingualism and translanguaging: Commonalities and divergences. *International Journal of Bilingual Education and Bilingualism*, *23*(1), 17–35. https://doi-org /10.1080/13670050.2019 .1598932

García, O., & Wei, L. (2013). *Translanguaging: Language, bilingualism and education*. Palgrave Macmillan.

Genesee, F. (2016). *At-risk learners and bilingualism: Is it a good idea?* ¡Colorín colorado! https://www.colorincolorado.org/article/risk-learners-and-bilingualism-it -good-idea

Goldin-Meadow, S. (1999). The role of gesture in communication and thinking. *Trends in Cognitive Sciences*, *3*(11), 419–429. https://doi.org/10.1016/S1364 -6613(99)01397-2

Goldin-Meadow, S. (2015). Gesture as a window onto communicative abilities: Implications for diagnosis and intervention. *Perspectives on Language Learning and Education*, *22*(2), 50–60. https://doi.org/10.1044/lle22.2.50

González, N., Moll, L., & Amanti, C. (2005). *Funds of knowledge: Theorizing practices in households, communities, and classrooms*. Erlbaum.

Grassroots Institute for Fundraising Training. (2012). *Grassroots Institute for Fundraising Training: Systems of power & oppression*.

Gutiérrez, K. D. (2024, September). Worldmaking for just educational futures: A utopian vision and methodology. World Educational Research Association (WERA) Keynote Lecture. Manchester, UK.

Hackett, A. (2021). *More-than-human literacies in early childhood*. Bloomsbury Publishing.

Hammond, T. (2023). *A day with no words.* Wheat Penny Press.

Harry, B., & Klingner, J. (2006). *Why are so many minority students in special education?: Understanding race & disability in schools.* Teachers College Press.

Henner, J., & Robinson, O. (2021). Unsettling languages, unruly bodyminds: Imaging a crip linguistics. Cornell University. https://doi.org/10.31234/osf.io/7bzaw

The Informed SLP. [@theinformedslp]. (2023, October 4). We've talked about the double empathy problem before—Both autistic and neurotypical people struggle to understand one another. [Instagram post].

Jakobson, R. (1961). *Linguistics and communications theory.* American Mathematical Society.

Kelley, R. D. G. (2002). *Freedom dreams: The Black radical imagination.* Beacon Press.

Kington, A., Gates, P., & Sammons, P. (2013). Development of social relationships, interactions and behaviours in early education settings. *Journal of Early Childhood Research, 11*(3), 292–311. https://doi.org/10.1177/1476718X13492936

Ladson-Billings, G. (1995). Toward a theory of culturally relevant pedagogy. *American Educational Research Journal, 32*(3), 465–491. https://doi.org/10.3102/00028312032003465

Lau v. Nichols, 414 U.S. 563 (1974).

MacLean, R. (2023). *More than Words: So Many Ways to Say What We Mean.* Henry Holt and Co.

Maturana, H. R. (1978). Biology of language: The epistemology of reality. In G. A. Miller & and E. Lenneberg (Eds.), *Psychology and biology of language and thought* (pp. 1–19). Academic Press.

Merriam-Webster. (2024). *Dumb.* https://www.merriam-webster.com/dictionary/dumb

Michigan Alliance for Families. (2024). Behavior is communication. Michigan Alliance for Families.

Miguel, J. & Padía, L. (in press). "They told us not to use Spanish": Linguistic ideologies & disabled bilingual youth. In J. Rios Vega & Y. Medina (Eds.), *LatCrit and education: Dismantling the norm while creating visibility.* Peter Lang.

Morin, A. (2024). *Understanding behavior as communication: A teacher's guide.* Understood.org. https://www.understood.org/en/articles/understanding-behavior-as-communication-a-teachers-guide

Nair, V. [@vishinair5]. (2022, October 26). *To me the term alternative & augmentative communication (AAC) is problematic. Alternative indicates everything else is alternative to oral lang.* [Post]. X [formerly Twitter]. https://x.com/vishinair5/status/1585314128763457537?s=21

Ortiz, A. A. (1984). Choosing the language of instruction for exceptional bilingual children. *Teaching Exceptional Children, 16*(3), 208–212. https://doi.org/10.1177/004005998401600311

Padía, L. (2020). Teaching safety, compliance, and critical thinking in special education classrooms. In S. Brand (Ed.), *Social justice and putting theory into practice in schools and communities* (pp. 227–244). IGI Global.

Padía, L. (2023). Toward a model of reciprocal carryover: Learning from communication systems of families of nonspeaking bilingual children. *Language, Speech, and Hearing Services in Schools, 54*(3), 716–728.

Padía, L. (2024). Student-driven individualized education program practice: Collaborating with young students as literacy learning agents. *Language Arts, 101*(3), 199–204. https://doi.org/10.58680/la202432767

Padía, L., & Traxler, R. E. (2020). (Special) Education is political; (Special) education is social justice. *Journal of Critical Thought and Praxis, 10*(1). https://doi.org/10.31274/jctp.11613

Padía, L., & Traxler, R. E. (2021). "We don't kiss in school": Policing warmth, disciplining physicality, and examining consent of Latinx students in U.S. special education classrooms. In D. Hernandez & C. Figueroa (Eds.), *Dis/ability in the Americas* (pp. 195–216. Palgrave Macmillan.

Paris, D. (2019). Naming beyond the white settler colonial gaze in educational research. *International Journal of Qualitative Studies in Education, 32*(3), 217–224. https://doi.org/10.1080/09518398.2019.1576943

Pedro-Carañana, J., Herrera-Huérfano, E., & Ochoa Almanza, J. (Eds.). (2022). *Communicative justice in the pluriverse: An international dialogue* (1st ed.). Routledge.

Pennycook, A. (2017). Translanguaging and semiotic assemblages. *International Journal of Multilingualism, 14*(3), 269–282. https://doi-org /10.1080/14790718.2017.1315810

Pérez, M. S. (2017). Black feminist thought in early childhood studies: (Re)Centering marginalized feminist perspectives. In K. Smith, K. Alexander, & S. Campbell (Eds.), *Feminism(s) in early childhood: Perspectives on children and young people* (Vol. 4, pp. 49–62). Springer.

Przymus, S. D., & Alvarado, M. (2019). Advancing bilingual special education: Translanguaging in content-based story retells for distinguishing language difference from disability. *Multiple Voices for Ethnically Diverse Exceptional Learners, 19*(1), 23–43.

Riggs, C. (2021). *Ask the expert: "Nonspeaking" vs. "nonverbal" and why language matters.* Guild for Human Services. https://www.guildhumanservices.org/blog/ask-expert-nonspeaking-vs-nonverbal-and-why-language-matters

Seidman, I. (2019). *Interviewing as qualitative research: A guide for researchers in education and the social sciences* (5th ed.)

Shakespeare, T. (2006). The social model of disability. *The Disability Studies Reader, 2*(3), 197–204.

Shannon, C. E. (1949). Communication in the presence of noise. *Proceedings of the IRE, 37*(1), 10–21.

Sins Invalid. (2018). *Principles of disability justice.* https://sinsinvalid.org/10-principles-of-disability-justice/

Sins Invalid. (2019). *Skin, tooth, and bone: The basis of movement is our people* (2nd ed.).

Snelgrove, S. (2005). Bad, mad and sad: Developing a methodology of inclusion and a pedagogy for researching students with intellectual disabilities. *International Journal of Inclusive Education, 9*(3), 313–329.

Souto-Manning, M., Martinez, D. C., & Musser, A. D. (2022). ELA as English language abolition: Toward a pedagogy of communicative belonging. *Reading Research Quarterly, 57*(4), 1089–1106. https://doi.org/10.1002/rrq.464

United States Department of Education. (2022). *OSEP fast facts: Students with disabilities who are English learners (ELs) served under IDEA Part B*. https://sites.ed.gov/idea/osep-fast-facts-students-with-disabilities-english-learners

Toppelberg, C. O., Snow, C. E., & Tager-Flusberg, H. (1999). Severe developmental disorders and bilingualism. *Journal of the American Academy of Child and Adolescent Psychiatry*, *38*(9), 1197–1199.

Wang, P., & Woolf, S. B. (2015). Trends and issues in bilingual special education teacher preparation: A literature review. *Journal of Multilingual Education Research*, 6(1), 35–59.

Yergeau, M. (2018). *Authoring autism: On rhetoric and neurological queerness*. Duke University Press.

Yosso, T. J. (2005). Whose culture has capital? A critical race theory discussion of community cultural wealth. *Race Ethnicity and Education*, 8, 69–91. https://dx.doi.org/10.1080/1361332052000341006

Yu, B. (2016). Bilingualism as conceptualized and bilingualism as lived: A critical examination of the monolingual socialization of a child with autism in a bilingual family. *Journal of Autism and Developmental Disorders, 46*, 424–435. https://doi.org/10.1007/s10803-015-2625-0

Index

A Day with No Words (Hammond), 133–134
Academia
  communication issues and, 20
  use of "racialized" term in, 21
  words accessorizing, 19
Adami, E., 49
Advocate/Ally, for family, 101
Ahenakew, C., 133
Alim, H. S., 8
Alsace, T., 42, 43
Alternative and augmentative communication (AAC) devices, 2, 9, 15
  bilingual programming, 29, 32
  English-only programming, 5–6, 50
  multimodal communication and, 48
  translanguaging and, 50
Alvarado, M., 8
Amanti, C., 72, 101
American Speech–Language–Hearing Association (ASHA), 46, 68, 112. *See also* Communication Bill of Rights
Annamma, S. A., 4, 40, 64
Antecedent-Behavior-Consequence (ABC) chart, 88, 124, 125
  CER checklist alternative to, 124, 126–128
Applied Behavior Analysis (ABA) therapy, 111
Arendt, H., 134
Arm-flapping. *See* "Stimming" actions
Artiles, A. J., 59
Authoring Autism (Yergeau), 26
Autism spectrum disorder, 5, 26
  IEP goals and, 36

@backendzyy, 23
Badwan, K., 133
Baker, C., 43
Baker-Bell, A., 37–38
Basic interpersonal communication skills (BICS), 72
Bauler, C. V., 3, 109
Behavior, as communication, 111–113
  daily/weekly reports on, 99–100
  development hierarchy, 48
  with intent, 26–27
  "stimming," 26–27
Behavioral Intervention Plans (BIPs), 107–108
Bernardo (minimally verbal bilingual child), 25
  expressed meaning example, 27
  family/teacher comments about, 64, 68, 70–71, 88–89, 113
  services received/language of service, 61
Bilingual/Bilingualism, 3
  cognitive systems and, 42
  conceptualization of, 109
  neurodivergent students and, 58
Bilingual Language and Literacy Investigative and Networking Group (BLLNG), 2
Bilingual/Multilingual education
  asset *vs.* deficit perspective and, 8–9
  cognitive burden and, 73
  counseling against, 134

Bilingual/Multilingual education (*continued*)
monolingual special education and, choosing between, 57–58
multimodal lessons and materials, 95, 102
myth of, 13, 59–60
nonverbal communication and, 36
positioning of, 58
Bilingual students, 2
biliterate/bilingual lives of, 58, 106–107
with disability. *See* Emergent bilinguals labeled as disabled (EMLADs)
emergent, studies on, 8, 68
marginalization of, 58
multimodal signs and, 50
nonspeaking. *See* Nonspeaking bilingual children
Black English, 37–38
Black Feminist Thought in Early Childhood Studies (Pérez), 24
Blommaert, J., 49
Body movements, 19, 26–27, 116, 135. *See also specific movement types*
Boveda, M., 4
Brady, N. C., 47, 102
Brea-Spahn, M. R., 2, 3, 109
British Educational Research Association (BERA), 133
Bruce, S., 47, 102

Campbell, C. C., 43
CAST, 58
Chee, A., 134
Child development, deficit perspective and, 6
Children
communication between, 10, 93–94, 115–116
relationships between, 94–95
as study participants, 24–25
Choice, bilingual *vs.* monolingual special education, 57–58
Cioè-Peña, M., 3, 9, 21, 44, 57, 62, 64, 102, 109
City University of New York–New York State Initiative on Emergent Bilinguals, 8, 68
Classrooms. *See* Communication communities
Code-switching, 42
Cognitive academic language proficiency (CALP), 72
Cognitive disability
bilingualism myth and, 59–60
language acquisition and, 6, 8
standardized metrics and, 59–60
Cognitive system, bilingualism and, 42
@_colenewberry, 21
Collaborative video use/analysis, 96–97
Collective commitment, communication and, 33–35
Colón, G., 42, 43
Common Core Standards, 6
Communication, x
between children, 10, 93–94, 115–116
claims about, 36
for collective commitment, 33–35
connection made through, ix
daily/weekly reports on, 99–100
devices supporting. *See* Alternative and augmentative communication (AAC) devices
flexible expectations/systems for, ix–x
functional, 94
misaligned modes/styles, 22
normative *vs.* expected form, 133
parent–child, 10
perspectives on, 36–37
practices. *See* Communicative practices/repertoires
recognizing forms of, 17–18, 135
rewiring, benefits of, 23, 123
structures/systems. *See* Communication structures/systems
understanding, positive benefits of, x
Communication Bill of Rights, 46–47, 50–51
classroom evaluation chart, 129–132
revisiting, 102–104

Communication communities, 1, 22–23, 82, 96, 124, 135, 136
ASHA communicative rights and, 129–132
culture of power and, 52–55, 95
desired characteristics, x
family involvement in (case studies), 84–89
holistic, 28–29, 136
perceptive partnerships and, 82, 110
practices in, 18–19
student self-evaluation in, 102–103, 104
Communication structures/systems
daily school occurrences (case studies), 92–93
independence *vs.* adult support at home/school (case studies), 89–90
multimodal/multisensory (case studies), 84–89
nonspeaking bilingual students and, 7, 19, 79–80. *See also* Kenny (minimally speaking bilingual student)
picture-based, 9, 15, 23–24
in student families/students, 59
"Communicative belonging," 124, 129
Communicative justice, 52–55. *See also* Communication Bill of Rights
communication communities and, 95–96
components in, 38–39
culture of power and (exercise), 53–54
enacting, 126
expansive linguistic repertoires protocol, 53–54, 55
freedom achieved through, 136
listening and, 49
need for, 24
nonspeaking emergent bilingual students and, 11–12
for nonspoken language, 122–123
planning for, 31–32
questions for power/oppression issues in, 74, 76
read-aloud example, 14–15
strategies for, 134
as third space/utopian project, 134
umbrella metaphor for, 37, 38
Communicative Justice in Action (CJA) Planning Tool, 28, 31–32, 53
Communicative practices/repertoires, 59
centering, 18–20
Expansive Linguistic Protocol, 52–55
home-to-school transfer of. *See* Reciprocal carryover
honoring and respecting all forms of, 105–106
impact of social interaction on, 46
negating, 59
of nonspeaking bilingual students, 6–7, 9, 106–107
translanguaging and. *See* Translanguaging
Communicative rights. *See* Communication Bill of Rights
Conditions-Expression-Response (CER) checklist, 124, 126–128
Connection, through communication, ix
Connor, D., 40, 64
Core boards. *See* Picture-based communication structures/systems
Crais, E., 43
Crip/"Cripping" linguistics
in communicative justice, 37, 38, 39–40
linguistic care work and, 81–82
raciolinguistic perspective and, 40
Crompton, C. J., 22
Cultural capital, 3
Culture of power
access to, 59
communicative justice and, 52–55
language use exercise, 54–55
rules of, 51–52
Cummins, J., 60, 72

Daily Mirror [@DailyMirror], 8, 20–21
Danesi, M., 36, 38
de Oliveira Andreotti, V., 133

Deficit ideologies/thinking, 22, 26
in languaging, challenges to, 36–37
skill *vs.* performance, 108
unpacking/transforming, 3, 136
Delpit, L., 51, 59, 81
Disability
author's relationship with, 4
bilingualism and, 58, 73
cognitive. *See* Cognitive disability
defined, 2
medical model of, 73, 116
Disability critical race theory (DisCrit), 40–41
Douglas, D. D., 43

Early intervention (EI), 60
Echolalia, 87, 88, 92
Education. *See also* Bilingual/Multilingual education; Special education
English-only. *See* English-only education
hospicing, 133
individual student plans. *See* Individualized Education Plans (IEPs)
language, 3
schooling *vs.*, 20
utopian projects in, 134
Education research/writing, 20, 73, 134–135
Educator team collaborations, 77
Ehlers-Zavala, F. P., 43
Emergent bilinguals (EBs), 9
Emergent bilinguals labeled as disabled (EMLADs), 2
consent/dissent interview protocols and, 100–101
language learning and, 9
nonspeaking/translanguaging student studies and, 8
Emergent multilinguals (EMs), 9
Emerson, R. M., 9, 99
Emmanual (nonspeaking bilingual child), 25
intervention services/language of service, 61, 92
lived realities of, 134
parent/caregiver comments about, 62–64, 85–86
quirks as intentions, 110–111
relationship with autistic classmate, 94–95
Emotion(s), expressions of, 86, 135
characteristics, 99
echolalia and, 88, 92
perceived as communication, 108, 112, 115
English language learners (ELLs), 7
deficit perspective and, 8–9
identifying, 135
labeling implications and, 2–3, 62
new names for, 9
English language proficiency, testing for, 57, 58
English-only education
AAC device programming and, 5–6, 50
facets of power/oppression in, 74, 75
Erickson, K., 47, 102
Ethnographic interviewing, 98–99, 136
bilingualism and special education, 74–76
Evans-Winters, V., 4
Expansive communication, 24
collective commitment and, 33–35
with pedagogical integrity (Venn diagram), 124, 129
presence/absence of, 19
read-aloud example, 14–15
use of visuals for, 49
Expansive Linguistic Repertoires Protocol, 52–55
Expression, modalities of, 18–19
Expressive language, intent to communicate and, 110
Eye contact/Eye gaze, 19, 135
cultural expectations and, 36

Facial expressions, 19, 70, 97, 106, 112
Familial communication systems, 13
characteristics, 83–84
educator responsiveness to, 96
educators learning from, 83

within family, 10
home-to-school transfer of. *See* Reciprocal carryover
languaging construction, 81
linguistic care work and, 82
nonspeaking bilingual children and, 6–7
Families
advocate/ally for, 101
educator interactions with, 136
experiences with bilingualism and special education, 74–76
as experts of own experience, 4–5, 90
freedom dreaming and, 3
funds of knowledge and, 101–102
home communication practices, 86
observation of, 99
as perceptive partners, 81, 84–89
as study participants, 24–25
Family questionnaires, inadequacy of, 83
Ferri, B., 40, 64
Flapping arms/hands, 26, 27, 112, 114
Fletcher-Watson, S., 22
Flores, N., 8, 20, 21, 36–37, 41, 72, 81
Flynn, E., 22
Four I's of Power and Oppression (framework), 74, 75
Freedom, communicative justice and, 136
Freedom dreaming, 3, 134
Fretz, R. I., 9, 99
Functional Behavioral Assessments (FBAs), 107–108
Functional communication, 94
Funds of knowledge
BICS and CALP distinction and, 72
family evaluation and, 101–102

García, E. S., 72
García, O., 8, 9, 11, 36–37, 49, 50
Gates, P., 46
Genesee, F., 9
Gestures/Gesturing, 19, 135
communicative justice and, 35, 38
development, 38, 48
with intent, 26–27
Goldin-Meadow, S., 26, 107, 114
Goldman, A., 47, 102
González, N., 72, 101
Google Translate, 49
Grassroots Institute for Fundraising Training, 74
Gutiérrez, K. D., 134

Hackett, A., 23
Hallett, S., 22
Hamer, Fannie Lou (activist), 18
Hammond, T., 133
Hand-flapping. *See* "Stimming" actions
Happiness Falls (Kim), 2
Harry, B., 9
Head-banging, 26
Head movements, communicating via, 84, 106, 116
Hector (minimally verbal child), 24–25
access to family/home language and, 45, 69
family/provider comments about, 37, 62, 65, 92–93, 111–113
friend as interlocutor for, 94
language skill growth in, 45
parental interaction with, 86–92
reciprocal carryover and, 93
schooling experience, 92
services received/language of, 61
WMSE use and, 46
Henner, J., 39–40, 81–82
Herrera-Huérfano, E., 37
Home Language Questionnaire (HLQ), 57, 62
Horton, Miles, 79
Hospicing, education and normative communication, 133
Hunt, D., 133

Identity. *See* Positioning/Positionality statements
Identity-first language, defined, 2
Ideological oppression, 74, 75
communicative justice and, 74, 76

Ideology(ies)
deficit. *See* Deficit ideologies/thinking
language/linguistic, 65–66, 115–122
professional training *vs.* family expertise, 83
raciolinguistic, 60
In-text citations, as communicative barriers, 20
Individualized Education Plans (IEPs), 7
accommodations in, 28–31, 102–104
English Language Proficiency exam and, 58
FBAs and BIPs supporting, 107–108
goals on, 7, 36
student-driven practice and, 28, 29, 97
student self-evaluation/self-reflection, 28–31, 102–104
updating schedule, 29
Individualized Family Service Plans (IFSPs), 7
The Informed SLP [@theinformedslp], 22
Institutional oppression, 74, 75
communicative justice and, 74, 76
Intent/Intention to communicate, 13–14
communicative justice and, 122–123
expressive language and, 110
inaccessible/unreadable by adults, 113–114
perceptive partners and, 107
quirks as, 110–111
whining as form of, 111–113
Internalized oppression, 74, 75
communicative justice and, 74, 76
Interpersonal oppression, 74, 75
communicative justice and, 74, 76
Inventive language/spelling, 27

Jakobson, R., 38
Justice
communicative. *See* Communicative justice
linguistic, steps toward, 59

Katrina (nonverbal bilingual child), 25
family/therapist comments about, 71–72, 117, 121, 122
services received/language of service, 61
Kelley, R. D. G., 3
Kenny (minimally speaking bilingual student), 79–80, 85–86, 87, 95, 101, 133, 135
Kim, Angie, *Happiness Falls,* 2
Kington, A., 46
Klingner, J., 9
Kress, G., 49
KWL self-reflection chart, IEP accommodations, 103–104

Labeling implications, 20–21, 39, 75
disabled students. *See* Emergent bilinguals labeled as disabled (EMLADs)
English language learners, 8–9, 62. *See also* Nasir (Black nonspeaking bilingual child)
stigma and, 62
Ladson-Billings, G., 8
Language
acquisition of, cognitive disability and, 6, 8
in classroom, 35–36
educator ideologies and, 115–122
embodied, culture and, 109
expressive and receptive, 5, 109–110
function of, rethinking, 108
inventive, spoken/unspoken, 27
named, AAC devices and, 5–6
pedagogy theories and, 13
policing, 23
re-imagining, x
reductive, 108
Language education, 3
"Language exploding," 45
"Language minoritized children," 49–50
Languaging
conceptualization of, 109
deficit thinking in, challenges to, 36–37
defined, 2
family co-construction for, 81
liberatory, 3
Larsen-Freeman, D., 49
LatDisCrit Dual Socialization (LDS), 90

Lau v. Nichols, 43
Lazarus, Emma (activist), 18
Learning communities/processes. *See* Communication communities
Liberatory languaging, 3
Linguistic care work, 81–82
Linguistic ideology, 65–66
Linguistic Justice (Baker-Bell), 37–38
Linguistic justice, steps toward, 59. *See also* Communicative justice
Listening
  communicative justice and, 49
  facial expressions and, 17, 21–22
  importance of, x
  rewiring, benefits of, 23, 123
Listening gaze/stance, 12
Literature, translanguaging and, 46

MacLean, Roz, 14–15
Marginalization
  of communication practices, 7
  language minoritized children and, 49–50
Martinez, D. C., 124
Maturana, H. R., 2
Meaning/Meaning-making
  children's own way of, 94
  expressive intent *vs.* receptive interpretation, 110
  multimodal/multilingual, 6
  translanguaging and, 8, 42
  unspoken layers of, x
Medicaid, bilingual SLPs and, 72
Merriam-Webster, 43–44
Metacognition, 51
Michigan Alliance for Families, 112
Miguel, J., 90
Mineo, B., 47, 102
Minimally verbal/speaking, 10
Moll, L., 72, 101
Monolingual special education/learning
  bilingual myth and, 60
  bilingualism and, choosing between, 57–58
  implications of, 58–59
More-Than-Human Literacies in Early Childhood (Hackett), 23
More Than Words: . . . (MacLean), 14–15, 135
Morin, A., 112
Multidirectional communication logs, 99–100
Multilingual education, 2. *See also* Bilingual/Multilingual education
Multilingual/Multilingualism, 2. *See also* Bilingual/Multilingual education
  emergent, 9
  intersection with multimodal communication, 46, 136
Multimodal communication/semiotics, 37, 38
  AAC devices and, 48
  active role in children's communication, 94
  culturally responsive-sustaining, 10, 28
  literature and, 46
  multilingualism intersection with, 46, 136
  multisensory systems and, 84–89
Musser, A. D., 124

Nair, V., 6
Named languages, AAC devices and, 5–6
Nasir (nonspeaking bilingual child)
  social boundaries and, 33–34, 38–39, 41, 135
  WMSE use and, 46, 47
Nathaniel (minimally speaking bilingual student), 105–106, 108, 115, 120, 135
Neurodivergent students, bilingualism and, 58
New York City Teaching Fellows program, 5
Newberry, C., 21
Next Generation Standards, 6
Niveyah (nonspeaking bilingual child), 24
  family/therapist comments about, 65–66, 84–85, 91, 115–121
  services received/language of service, 61
Nonspeaking (no verbal output), 1–2

Nonspeaking bilingual children
bilingual lives of, 58, 106–107
communicative justice and, 11–12, 136
communicative practices of. *See* Communicative practices
education research on, 3–4, 134–136. *See also* Emergent bilinguals labeled as disabled (EMLADs)
educators' language ideologies with, 115–122
future directions, 134
perceptive partners and, 109
school communication structures and, 7
translanguaging studies and, 9
Nonspeaking multilingual students, white listening subject perception of, 21–22
Nonverbal, nonspeaking and
distinction between, 2
intention and, 119
Nonverbal communication, cultural expectations and, 36
Normative communication, hospicing of, 133

Occupational therapy (OT), 92
Ochoa Almanza, J., 37
Ogletree, B. T., 47, 102
Oppression, "Four I's" of, 74, 75
Ordinariness, notion of, 23
visual aids and, 23–24
Ortiz, A. A., 59, 60
Otheguy, R., 36–37, 50

Padía, L., 28, 41, 46, 74, 80, 81, 87, 90, 98, 101, 103, 107, 109, 129
Paris, D., 3, 8
Pedagogy
educators and, 44, 68, 74, 95, 96
individual language development and, 6
integrity of, expansive communication with (Venn diagram), 124, 129
of perception, 72, 82, 86, 95, 96, 107, 123, 135, 136
Pedro-Carañana, J., 37
Pennycook, A., 50
Perception
pedagogy of, 72, 82, 86, 95, 96, 107, 123, 135, 136
rewiring, benefits of, 23, 123 ??find all perceive and percept??
Perceptive partners/partnerships
becoming, 22, 93, 97
communication communities and, 82, 110
communicator's intention and, 107
families as, 81
nonspeaking bilingual children and, 109
rewiring, 120, 123
Pérez, M. S., 24
Person-first language, 2
Picture-based communication structures/systems, 9, 15, 23–24
Picture Exchange Communication system (PECS), 121
Pointing (gesture), cultural differences and, 19
Positioning/Positionality statements, 4
Power. *See also* Oppression
culture of, 51. *See also* Culture of power
raciolinguistic perspective and, 21
Power dynamics, 4
"Prohibited Classroom Words" list, 23
Przymus, S. D., 8

Race, as social construct, 21
"Racialized," significance of term, 21
Raciolinguistic ideology, 60
Raciolinguistics/Raciolinguistic perspective
bilingual myth and, 60
in communicative justice, 38, 41–42
concept/significance of terms, 19–20
crip linguistics and, 40
impact on communication, 20–22
intention to communicate and, 119
Ratcliffe, T., 133
Receptive language, interpretation and, 110

Reciprocal carryover, 13, 80–82
caregiver–educator, 90, 91
case studies, 84–89
communicative justice and, 96
strategies, 98–99
Reductive language, 108
Relationships, between children, 94–95
Riggs, C., 2
Rights. *See* Communication Bill of Rights
Robinson, O., 39–40, 81–82
Rocking back and forth, 26, 112, 113, 114, 118, 137
Ropar, D., 22
Rosa, J., 8, 20, 21, 36–37, 41, 81
Roy, Arundhati, 1, 14, 105

Sammons, P., 46
Schooling, education *vs.*, 20
Schools/School system
communication structures in, 7
identifying power and oppression in, 74, 75
positioning of/assumptions about, 3
preoccupation of, 6
Seidman, I., 8
Seltzer, K., 36–37
Shakespeare, T., 116
Shannon, C. E., 38
Shared Video Reflection Protocol, 96–97, 98
Shaw, L. L., 9, 99
Sherris, A., 49
Sins Invalid, 3, 48
Skill *vs.* performance deficits, 108
"Slang," 23
Snelgrove, S., 100
Snow, C. E., 73
Social class, raciolinguistic perspective and, 20–21
Social interaction, communicative development and, 46
Social media, 22
Social signs/semiotics, 49
literature and, 46
Souto-Manning, M., ix–x, 124
on schooling *vs.* education, 20
Special education, 2
bilingualism *vs.* monolingual, choosing between, 57–59
program (District 75, NYC), 5
translanguaging studies and, 8
Speech and Language Impairment (SLI), 7
Speech language pathologist (SLP)
bilingual, 72–73, 109, 119
on cultural perspective of family and child, 68–69
on students' language development, 116, 117, 118–119, 122
Speech language pathology, misaligned modes/styles and, 22
Speech providers, teachers collaborating with, 77
Spinning in circles, 26, 114, 127
Spoken language, as humanity marker, 26
"Standard academic English," academic achievement and, 26
Stein, S., 133
Stigma, 62
subverting (case example), 95
"Stimming" actions, 26–27, 116, 135
Student Agency in Communication (SAC), 28–30
electronic greeting choice boards and, 51
Student-driven Individualized Education Program Practice (SIP), 28, 29, 97
Student self-evaluation/self-reflection, IEP accommodations, 28–31, 102–103, 104
Students
learning process and, 32
self-evaluation tools, 28–31, 102–103, 104

Tager-Flusberg, H., 73
Talking, beyond verbal ways, 21
Teacher(s)
professional development for, 135
rewiring own perceptive skills, 123
speech provider collaborations with, 77
as white listening subject, 21

Teaching in Action, x
bilingual/nonspeaking students, raciolinguistics and, 74–77
culture of power and communicative justice, 52–55
family–educator collaboration, 96–104
More Than Words: . . . (MacLean), 14–15
student intentional communication, resources/tools for, 123–132
student self-monitoring/self-evaluation, 28–31
Technology, communication benefits and detriments, 90–91
Think-Pair-Share activities, 32
Third spaces, as utopian projects, 134
Toppelberg, C. O., 73
Translanguaging, 2, 42. *See also* TrUDL (translanguaging and universal design for learning)
in communicative justice, 38, 42
multimodal, 59
nonspeaking bilingual students and, 9
traditional linguistic//psychological theories and, 8
Traxler, R. E., 41, 46, 101
TrUDL (translanguaging and universal design for learning), 102–104
in communicative justice, 37, 38, 44–45

Universal Design for Learning (UDL), translanguaging and. *See* TrUDL (translanguaging and universal design for learning)
Unspoken voice, 27
U.S. Department of Education, 7
Utopian projects, in education, 134

Verbal/Nonverbal, 2
nonverbal and nonspeaking distinguished, 2
speaking/listening expansion beyond, 21
Veronica (minimally verbal student), 17–18, 21, 53, 135
Video
capturing student behaviors, 92–93
communication with families via, 136
notes/messages via, platforms supporting, 100
Shared Video Reflection Protocol, 96–97, 98
Visuals/Visual aids. *See also* Picture-based communication structures/systems
electronic greeting choice boards, 51
lesson accessibility and, 49
ordinariness and, 23–24
Voice/"Voice"
AAC devices and, 2, 6
unspoken, 27

Walker, Camille, 33
Wang, P., 43
Wei, L., 8, 9, 36–37
Whining, as form of intention, 111–113
White listening subject
educator's role as, 81
perception beyond spoken English word, 94
raciolinguistic perspective and, 41–42
White mainstream spoken English (WMSE), 23
decentering, 38, 59, 74, 75, 133–134
destabilizing strategies, 134
failure to communicate with, 46, 47
steps toward linguistic justice and, 59
Wilkinson, K., 47, 102
Woolf, S. B., 43
Word(s)
approximation of, 49
prohibited in classroom, list of, 23
World Educational Research Association (WERA), 133
Wright, W. E., 43
Writing, as verbal act, 2

Yergeau, M., 26, 116
Yosso, T. J., 3
Yu, B., 9

About the Author

Lilly Padía is an assistant professor of raciolinguistic justice in early childhood teacher education at Erikson Institute in Chicago. Her scholarship and community work explore liberation for children, families, and communities through the intersections of disability, language, and race. Her work has been published in journals such as *Race Ethnicity and Education; Language, Speech and Hearing Services in Schools; Journal of Critical Study of Communication and Disability;* and *Theory Into Practice.*